ANTI-NIETZSCHE

ANTI-NIETZSCHE

MALCOLM BULL

VERSO

London • New York

This paperback edition first published by Verso 2014
First published by Verso 2011
© Malcolm Bull 2011, 2014

1 3 5 7 9 10 8 6 4 2

Verso
UK: 6 Meard Street, London W1F 0EG
US: 20 Jay Street, Suite 1010, Brooklyn, NY 11201

www.versobooks.com

Verso is the imprint of New Left Books

ISBN-13: 978-1-78168-316-3 (PBK)
eISBN-13: 978-1-78168-390-3 (UK)
eISBN-13: 978-1-84467-893-8 (US)

British Library Cataloguing in Publication Data
A catalogue record for this book is available from the British Library

Library of Congress Cataloging-in-Publication Data
A catalog record for this book is available from the Library of Congress

Typeset in Fournier by Hewer Text UK Ltd, Edinburgh
Printed in the US by Maple Press

Contents

Foreword

This book belongs to the many, to anybody in fact—which means, of course, that it belongs to no one.

What if the world itself were like that? For Nietzsche, the sense of the world does not lie outside the world but rather within the world, where (as Wittgenstein puts it) 'everything is as it is, and everything happens as it does happen'. If the sense of the world lies inside the world, then the meaning of the world can only be given by the things in it—their meaning its meaning. That is another way of saying that the meaning of the world is a question of population, and that arguments about its meaning must be determined through its demography and ecology.

If the sense of the world lies within it, nonsense lies without. If the world loses meaning, then that can only be because nonsense has taken the place of sense. The nonsense of the world, too, must be determined through its demography and ecology. Nietzsche calls the process through which nonsense comes into the world nihilism and attributes it to the 'slave revolt in morals'. Seeking to complete the process, and so bring nihilism to an end, Nietzsche describes an ecology in which the nonsense of the world is as it is forever.

The argument of this book is that Nietzsche's solution, far from being the completion of nihilism, is merely an attempt to arrest it. By excluding any future exchange of nonsense for sense, he also excludes any further exchange of sense for nonsense. Yet if, as Nietzsche himself asserts, such exchanges are ultimately just changes in the population of the world, his particular ecology can always be undermined by one that is more negative still. Why then does Nietzsche's nihilism still function as the limit-philosophy of the modern imaginary? This book suggests that there can be no humanist response to Nietzsche that does not augment rather than diminish the meaning of the world. Any ecology more negative than Nietzsche's must be a subhuman one, for only where nihilism moves beyond scepticism to failure does it fall below the reach of the transcendental arguments that turn nonsense back into sense.

Positive ecologies generate their own political meanings, but a negative ecology is an invitation to political theory. As Hobbes was perhaps the first to realise, political theory is a theory of populations without meanings, needed whenever the world loses some of its sense. That is why Nietzsche himself becomes a political theorist. The corollary of this is that political theory becomes impossible without nonsense. Is there some way to let the sense escape from Nietzsche's world? Suffocated by meanings we cannot understand, we must circle its limits looking for an opening, the crack that will let the nonsense in.

Acknowledgements

Earlier versions of some chapters were first published or presented elsewhere: chapters 1 and 2 in *New Left Review*; chapters 3 and 4 at the Townsend Center for the Humanities at Berkeley, and chapter 3 in *The Townsend Papers in the Humanities*; chapter 7 to the Seminar in Political Thought and Intellectual History at Cambridge. I am particularly grateful to my respondents on these occasions—T. J. Clark, Henry Staten, Judith Butler, and Anthony J. Cascardi at Berkeley, and Raymond Geuss in Cambridge—and also to my editors at *New Left Review*, Robin Blackburn, Perry Anderson, and Susan Watkins. At various points along the way encouragement has come from, among others, Julian Stallabrass, Barry Schwabsky, Gopal Balakrishnan, and Timothy Morton. My greatest debts are, as always, to Jill Foulston.

1

Philistinism

At last the horizon appears free to us again, even if it should not be bright; at last our ships may venture out again, venture out to face any danger; all the daring of the lover of knowledge is permitted again; the sea, our sea, lies open again; perhaps there has never yet been such an 'open sea'.

Nietzsche

Believing that philistinism was not mere vulgarity but 'the antithesis par excellence of aesthetic behaviour', Adorno expressed interest in studying the phenomenon as a *via negativa* to the aesthetic.[1] But the project remained unrealised, and although he frequently made dismissive or insulting remarks about philistines, he never bothered to investigate what, if anything, philistinism might be. In this respect, his attitude was characteristic of the discourse against philistinism that had been in circulation since the nineteenth century. Nevertheless, in his unfulfilled desire to study the philistine, Adorno opened the way to a revaluation of that tradition, for upon closer examination the philistine proves to be a figure of greater historical and intellectual importance than Adorno imagined.

On the face of it, the type of study Adorno had in mind should be relatively straightforward. A glance at the newspapers suggests that we are surrounded by philistines. We live, according to the critic D. J. Taylor, 'in a philistine age', and have, as another commentator noted the previous day, 'a government of philistines'.[2] No wonder,

therefore, that controversialists like Frank Furedi have set themselves the challenge of 'confronting twenty-first-century philistinism'.[3]
Yet it is not only the twenty-first century or the Conservative
government that are branded as philistine. In the previous decade,
the editor of *Tribune* was quoted as saying: 'There's a new philistinism in Labour',[4] and the *Literary Review* devoted an issue to a
'Cry Against the Philistines', a litany of protests against what
Tariq Ali, one of the contributors, called the 'commercial philistinism which has swamped this country's culture'.[5] According to
George Walden, another contributor, 'Philistines . . . are no
longer barbarians encamped outside the Citadel of the Arts: now
they sit atop it, benevolent-eyed, directing the cultural traffic.'[6]

Perhaps such protests should lead us to conclude that philistinism is something endemic to ruling classes. This was certainly the
view of one contributor to the letters pages of *Opera* magazine,
who concluded that: 'If there is such a thing as "the English
disease", it is, I submit, Philistinism in high places.'[7] But other
readers were quick to point out that he had underestimated the
extent of the problem. One responded that philistinism is an 'affliction [that] is widespread, insidious and in outward appearance not
always immediately recognizable'; philistinism is not confined to
high places but is, he argued, an 'infection [that] goes right down
to the roots of English life'.[8] Nevertheless, those with a less parochial perspective affirm that philistinism is not merely an English
disease: England may be rooted in philistinism, but by all accounts
its full flowering has taken place elsewhere, in what Terry Eagleton
has termed that 'extravagantly philistine country', the United States.[9]

Like Adorno, who believed that the philistine's 'anti-artistic
attitude verges on sickness',[10] contemporary critics of philistinism
treat the phenomenon as pathological. But what exactly is the
nature of the disease? To answer this question it is helpful to
employ a set of distinctions developed by Michael Thompson in
Rubbish Theory. According to his analysis there are three types of
object—those like antiques and works of art which are considered

durable and whose value is expected to increase; those that are considered transient (that is, everyday objects whose values are highest when new and subsequently decrease); and those that have no value and are treated accordingly.[11] Thompson's analysis allows us to define the philistine position more precisely. The philistine should argue not that existing objects are of temporary as opposed to durable aesthetic value, or that, although they may once have been or may yet become valuable, all existing objects are valueless, but that all objects are permanently aesthetically valueless. In consequence, any object whose value is derived solely from its classification as an art-object is fit only for recycling. With this in mind, it is easy to see that certain positions that are sometimes described as philistine are not really philistine at all. For example, people who value popular culture in the same way as high culture, or who prefer popular culture to high culture, are just promoting the transient at the expense of the durable or revaluing the transient as durable.

The position of anti-art movements like Dada is less clear. Dada certainly gave expression to the philistine impulse, but although its rhetoric was vigorously anti-aesthetic, what actually happened in the creation of a ready-made was that something that had the transient aesthetic value of a machine-produced object or was even an object of no value at all was then treated as though it were a durable object of lasting aesthetic value. It is therefore misleading to suggest that the ready-made says 'art is junk';[12] what it says is only that 'junk is art'. To demonstrate that art is junk, Dada would have had to work in the opposite direction. Duchamp certainly contemplated this: 'At another time, wanting to expose the basic antinomy between art and "ready-mades", I imagined a reciprocal ready-made: use a Rembrandt as an ironing board'.[13] However, neither he nor the other Dadaists did so, and the museums of the world were never turned into laundry rooms. In consequence, although art galleries are now filled with objects that might have been taken from rubbish tips, rubbish tips remain barren of objects taken from art galleries. Treating junk as art differs from treating art as junk in just the same way that pantheism differs from atheism, or a multi-culturalist respect for all moralities differs from the nihilist disregard for any morality. One is an inclusive extrapolation of value, the other its direct negation.

If philistinism is the absolute negation of the aesthetic, and is differentiated from the promiscuous pan-aestheticism of Dada and the temporalised aesthetics of popular culture, it becomes easier to see precisely what type of territory the philistines should occupy. Philistines are not just opposed to art for art's sake but have no time for the arts whatsoever. They never distinguish between a good tune and an awful one; they pass through areas of outstanding natural beauty without noticing; they are indifferent to their furniture; they never spot a masterpiece in a junk shop, or complain about the 'rubbish' in modern art galleries. For them, it is all rubbish. Indeed, the idea that other people might discern aesthetic differences between objects and evaluate them accordingly would seem intrinsically absurd. They might therefore also flout the expectation that they should behave differently in the presence of these aesthetically valued objects. They would drop litter in beauty spots, lean nonchalantly against the paintings in the National Gallery, demolish their listed homes, talk loudly to their neighbours during concerts.

There are, of course, many people who occasionally exhibit philistine behaviour, but they are rarely ideologically motivated, and when one investigates the ideological position the philistines supposedly occupy it proves surprisingly empty. Philistinism, for all its supposed ubiquity, is frustratingly elusive. Dictionaries of theology contain entries on atheism, and dictionaries of politics provide information about anarchism, but dictionaries of aesthetics contain no entries on philistinism.[14] There are no books on its principles,[15] no courses available at universities, and no Societies for the Promotion of Philistinism working with the public; there are not even any branches of Philistines Anonymous for those in recovery from the disease. If confronted, supposed philistines invariably argue that they are not actually philistines at all, just people opposed to the waste of public money, or some other social evil. They are, they say, not opposed to art per se, but simply to art that is offensive, or wasteful, or unrepresentative of the general population.

Is Philistinism Possible?

Any attempt to study philistinism must first take account of the curious fact that a constant stream of abuse is directed against philistinism without there being any self-identified philistines to whom these denunciations refer. How is this to be explained? The apparent absence of philistines from the cultural landscape might lead one to suppose that philistinism is not just a rare phenomenon but an imaginary one, and some would argue that if philistines are people who look upon all cultural products as valueless, they cannot exist. The argument for the imperative of value (used by Steven Connor), or the principle of generalised positivity (formulated by Barbara Herrnstein Smith), goes like this: to deny the value of everything is, if that denial is to carry any conviction, necessarily to value the denial itself. Therefore, as Smith argues in her critique of Bataille's notion of absolute expenditure, 'no valorization of anything, even of "loss" itself, can escape the idea of some sort of positivity—that is gain, benefit or advantage—in relation to some economy'.[16] In which case, the total renunciation of value is impossible, for all that is happening is that one set of values is being exchanged for another.

Applied to philistinism, this argument suggests that insofar as 'challenges to the structures of artistic value and value in general will themselves constitute forms of value, they will be promptly restored to the fields of exchange and transaction which they had attempted to transcend'.[17] Smith and Connor conceive of the discourse of value on the model of Derridean *différance*, as an economy of 'recurrent tautologies, circularities and infinite regresses' in which the negative is always eventually transmuted into the positive, and the most that negation can effect is 'the widening of the circuit which rounds negativity home to the positive eventualities of value'.[18] But although there are certainly instances in which what appears to be philistinism is not a renunciation of the aesthetic but an aesthetic of renunciation, there are also other possibilities. The aesthetic is only one among many forms of value, and philistinism only one of the ways of renunciation. It is quite conceivable that the denial of the aesthetic may be motivated not so much by an aesthetic of negation as by some non-aesthetic value. The renunciation of the aesthetic may be a moral, religious, or political imperative, just as the negation of these other spheres may have an aesthetic motivation: one could be, on aesthetic grounds alone, a nihilist, an atheist, or an anarchist. Such transfers from one type of value to another may not transcend evaluation altogether, but nor are they necessarily part of an inescapable circle from which no values are ever lost. So, even if one accepts the logic of the argument, the principle of general positivity, as it is misleadingly termed, demonstrates not the ubiquity of value but only its ineradicability. As such, it amounts to no more than a 'principle of general wetness' which states that in order to be described as such even the driest environment must have spots that are relatively moist. The existence of traces of value in the wastes of the negative does not imply that positivity is either predominant or constant. Not only may the level of the positive fluctuate, but certain types of value may evaporate entirely, only to be replaced by others. Indeed, the difficulty of upholding more than one type of value simultaneously suggests that the positive is never likely to be more than a tiny oasis in the vast expanses of the negative.

Thus, although value may be ineradicable, it may also be fragile, and its existence in any one area a contingent historical fact dependent on local conditions. The imperative of value therefore signals not the omnipresence of value, but the capacity of value to adapt and re-emerge at the very moment when it seemed to have disappeared. With this in mind, it is worth asking whether the fact that philistinism is a form of negation that is universally condemned but nowhere visible may be less a sign of its inescapable spectrality than a historically significant indication of the nature and location of positive value in contemporary society.

A Short History of Negation

Once upon a time, before nihilists and anarchists had been invented and when Philistines were just a tribe mentioned in the Old Testament, the only type of negation that anyone could imagine was the denial of the existence of God. Even so, 'atheism', although known to the ancient Greeks, is a word that enters modern European languages only in the sixteenth century.[19] Before that nobody seemed able to conceive of the possibility that such a direct negation of socially sanctioned values was possible. All deviants were classified as heretics—people whose negation of Christianity was itself a diabolical form of Christianity rather than people who negated the value of Christianity altogether. And even when atheism was isolated from heresy as a distinct category, it was not a word used by unbelievers to identify themselves, but by theologians to attack supposed unbelievers.

The position of atheism in early modern Europe has been extensively studied in recent years and offers striking analogies to the position of philistinism today. Atheists were perceived to be so numerous as to plague entire countries. According to one recent historian, 'To judge by . . . the learned literature of the age, "the atheist" was almost everywhere in early modern France';[20] but not only France: Guy Patin complained that 'Italy is a country of pox, poisoning and atheism';[21] Thomas Fuller echoed many other writers in believing that 'Atheisme in England is more to be feared than Popery'.[22] As Francis Bacon recognised, such indiscriminate use of the term made atheists seem more numerous than they were, but even he had no doubt that atheism was a real threat: 'They that deny a God destroy man's nobility; for certainly man is of kin to the beasts by his body; and if he be not of kin to God by his spirit, he is a base and ignoble creature.'[23]

Like philistinism, atheism was universally decried as a form of intellectual self-mutilation: according to Laurent Pollot, atheists must have 'gouged out their own eyes expressly in order not to see God in his works nor in his word'.[24] Indeed, atheism was viewed as so perverse that many commentators insisted that it was logically inconceivable. And even if that possibility were conceded, it could still be argued that a society of atheists would collapse under its own contradictions. Few joined Pierre Bayle in suggesting that a society of atheists might be viable.[25] So at the same time that atheism was everywhere denounced, its existence was held to be impossible. As Hume later remarked: 'There is not a greater number of philosophical reasonings displayed upon any subject, than those, which prove the existence of a Deity, and refute the fallacies of Atheists; and yet most religious philosophers still dispute whether any man can be so blinded as to be a speculative atheist.'[26]

Even if atheism were not—as Lucien Febvre claimed—conceptually impossible until the seventeenth century, there can be little doubt that at the time atheists were first denounced from the pulpits and burnt at the stake, there were hardly any atheists at all. The unfortunate people condemned as atheists were often those whose enthusiasm for denouncing this hypothetical crime was just insufficiently enthusiastic.[27] In the sixteenth century, therefore, atheism, like philistinism today, was everywhere condemned but nowhere to be found. Yet by denouncing atheism, theologians mapped out an intellectual position for their phantom adversaries that was eventually filled by people who actually espoused the arguments the theologians had given them.[28] Even so, it was a century after the word originated that the first indisputable modern atheists appeared, and well into the eighteenth century before atheism became commonplace.

But at the same time that atheism became a reality, people began to find values not in religion but in human society itself, and a new form of negation became imaginatively possible—anarchism. Like atheism, it emerges as the imaginary antithesis of the prevailing mode of value, except that in this case it is the antithesis of the state. Although first used as a term of abuse to describe religiously motivated libertarians in mid-seventeenth-century England, the meaning of 'anarchist' was not immediately differentiated from 'atheist', for atheism was, as Bacon put it, living 'without having respect to the government of the world'.[29] As late as 1678, Cudworth could dismiss the possibility that the Egyptians had been 'Atheists and Anarchists, such as supposed no living under-standing Deity' in favour of the idea that they might have been 'Polyarchists such as asserted a multitude of understanding deities'.[30] Nevertheless, the concepts of anarchism and atheism had already been prised apart. Irrespective of whether Hobbes was, as his critics invariably claimed, himself an atheist, he unquestionably gave priority to political rather than religious values, and in *Leviathan* (1651) subjected all religions, including Christianity, to the authority of the civil sovereign.[31] The negation against which he developed his argument in *Leviathan* was therefore anarchistic, not atheistic, and in his account of 'the time men live without a common Power to keep them all in awe' he offers a description of anarchism—first defined in Thomas Blount's *Glossographia* (1656) as 'the Doctrine, Positions or art of those that teach Anarchy; also the being itself of the people without a Prince or Ruler'—which ascribes to it the same dehumanizing consequences that Bacon had attributed to atheism: the absence of morality, and a life that is brutish and short.[32]

By providing 'the main theoretical basis for Restoration of atheism',[33] and, in his account of 'the state of Warre', a new negation against which the values necessary for a full human life might be defined, Hobbes effected a momentous transposition of values. One negation was tacitly accepted, and its negative implications transferred to another as a new value assumed priority. But just as the invention of atheism had taken place without anyone actually advocating the position, so the invention and repudiation of anarchism occurred without the intervention of any anarchists. No one espoused an explicitly anarchist political theory until William Godwin, and no one used 'anarchy' in a positive sense until Proudhon.[34] However, that did not prevent anarchists being roundly abused, and the French Revolution in particular provided numerous occasions for the denunciation of anarchism as the epitome of negativity and criminality: in 1791 Bentham wrote, '*Whatever is, is not*—is the maxim of the anarchist, as often as anything comes across him in the shape of a law he happens not to like';[35] four years later, the Directory put it more graphically: anarchists were 'men covered with crimes, stained with blood, and fattened by rapine, enemies of laws they do not make and of all governments in which they do not govern'.[36] Nevertheless, events in France also inspired the development of a political theory which embodied the anarchistic principles its critics denounced. And when they finally emerged to occupy the position so long ascribed to them, anarchists defined their philosophy by separating the political from the ethical. Thus, Godwin anticipated with delight 'the dissolution of political government . . . that brute engine which has been the only perennial cause of the vices of mankind',[37] but only because government so often proved to be 'the treacherous foe of the domestic virtues'.[38] Morality did not depend upon some form of social contract, but was 'an irresistible deduction from the wants of one man, and the ability of another to relieve them'.[39]

Although early anarchist thinkers like Godwin and Proudhon attacked the state on ethical grounds, it seemed to many observers that the anarchist spirit of negation would encompass all forms of morality. The nihilist was born. First used in this sense in a French dictionary of neologisms in 1801, a nihilist was defined as 'One who does not believe in anything'.[40] Needless to say, at this stage there was no one claiming to be a nihilist, just a chorus of outraged moralists arguing that nihilism disregards 'the highest motives and also the duties imposed by right and honour' and so signalled the start of a Hobbesian 'battle of all against all'.[41] However, self-proclaimed nihilists did eventually emerge in Russia. Although similar to anarchists, they saw themselves as reacting not so much 'against political despotism, but against the moral despotism that weighs upon the private and inner life of the individual'.[42] Nevertheless, in the numerous anti-nihilist novels of the 1860s, and even in Turgenev's more equivocal *Fathers and Sons*, nihilists were presented as indiscriminately hostile to everything.

This was not a portrayal that nihilists welcomed. Even those who accepted the label objected to the idea that they negated all values, arguing that 'when a person negates utterly everything he negates precisely nothing'.[43] And one charge they were particularly keen to deny was the idea that they were indifferent to the arts. Turgenev's nihilist Bazarov had dismissed Raphael, and in Krestovsky's anti-nihilist novel *Panurge's Head*, the nihilists argue that 'A normally developed and free people has no art and should have none. And if you produce art you should either be put in a mental hospital or a reformatory'.[44] But actual nihilists like Chernyshevsky refused to accept that they were philistines who 'reject everything . . . paintings, statues, violin and bow, opera, theatre, feminine beauty'.[45]

In Nietzsche, who derived his conception of nihilism from these Russian sources, the differentiation of nihilism from philistinism was taken much further. Although he welcomed the devaluation of all moral values, Nietzsche invested the aesthetic with heightened significance. He accepted 'the absolute untenability of existence when it comes to the highest values one recognises', but argued that 'it is only as an aesthetic phenomenon that existence and the world are eternally justified'.[46] As he later wrote in *Ecce Homo*, aesthetic values were 'the only values the Birth of Tragedy recognises'.[47] Yet again, the disappearance of value from one sphere was accompanied by its reappearance in another.

Nihilism was not, therefore, necessarily the end of all negativity. As Donoso Cortès remarked in 1851, 'The rejection of all authority is far from being the last of all possible negations; it is simply a preliminary negation which future nihilists will consign to their prolegomena'.[48] With the transfer of value from the moral to the aesthetic, a new form of negation did become possible—philistinism, the negation of the aesthetic, and it was at precisely the time nihilists emerged in Russia that the assault on philistinism began. The German word *philister* had been used in the eighteenth century to designate townspeople as opposed to students, but was subsequently applied to all those who were indifferent to the arts, first being used in this sense by Goethe.[49] In the 1830s, attacks on German philistines became commonplace—the members of Schumann's imaginary Davidsbund were enjoined to 'kill the philistines, musical and otherwise'[50]—and in 1869 the most famous polemic against philistinism appeared, Matthew Arnold's *Culture and Anarchy*.

This brief survey of the history of negation suggests that the contemporary position of philistinism as a negation that is everywhere condemned and nowhere advocated is both more interesting and less paradoxical than it first appears. Rather than being a constant within human history, the aesthetic is just the residuum left by the previous history of negation, and philistinism its corresponding but as yet unrealised negative. Atheism was identified and condemned from the sixteenth century onwards, but atheists appeared only in the seventeenth. Anarchists were abused from the seventeenth century and eventually materialised at the end of the eighteenth. But when anarchists emerged, a new spectre was born, the nihilist; and a generation later nihilists proclaimed their own existence. It is at exactly this moment that the philistine comes into being as the most recent but surely not the last negation.

The pattern that emerges from this series of negations is not circular but dialectical. Although each negation has eventually moved from spectrality to reality, it has not been incarnated in the form of its contrary. (Atheists did not set up a religion, anarchists did not form a government, and nihilists did not establish a morality.) Instead, the negation of one value allowed the differentiation and affirmation of another value that had been subsumed within it. At each new stage, ideological positions that had once appeared self-contradictory suddenly became available. The critics of atheism had assumed that there could be no political authority without God; the critics of anarchy argued that there could be no morality without the state; the critics of nihilism suggested that there could be no beauty without morality; and yet with each shift improbable new types appeared: the authoritarian atheist, the ethical anarchist, the aesthetic nihilist.

Set within this historical context, the invisibility of the philistines seems predictable. Throughout the sequence of negations, the absent negative is defined as a subhuman inversion of the primary value in the prevailing system, and one reason that negative positions are so slow to be filled is that occupying them is sometimes dangerous, often illegal, and always profoundly socially unacceptable. Today, of course, atheism, anarchism, and even nihilism are recognizable intellectual positions, and these terms have largely fallen out of favour as terms of abuse. But the very fact that people continue to call one another philistines, while refusing to accept the label themselves, is a clear sign that the aesthetic is assumed to be a shared social value and that being considered a philistine remains a potential embarrassment.[51] However, the historical pattern also suggests that the philistine position, having first been defined by its opponents, will eventually be occupied by its adherents. To find out what the philistine may be like, we must turn to its critics.

The Birth of Philistinism

Culture and Anarchy remains the classic statement of the opposition between culture and philistinism. But while Arnold declined to give a label to the adherents of culture, referring to them only as persons led 'by a general humane spirit, by the love of human perfection',[52] he differentiated between three groups in which the benefits of culture were imperfectly realised, absent, or rejected: the barbarians, the populace, and the philistines. The barbarians were those aristocrats who, instead of imbibing what Arnold termed the 'sweetness and light' of culture, had 'a kind of image or shadow of sweetness' formed from a superficial acquaintance with culture which left them with only 'the exterior graces and accomplishments, and the more external of the inward virtues'.[53] The populace were what Arnold termed 'that vast portion . . . of the working class which, raw and half-developed, has long lain half-hidden amidst its poverty and squalor',[54] while the philistines were those who were 'particularly stiff-necked and perverse in the resistance to light'.[55] They alone have no excuse. The populace are insensible to sweetness and light because they are deprived of it; the barbarians are seduced by 'exterior goods', but they are still goods, and to be seduced by them is natural. The philistines, however, cherish 'some dismal and illiberal existence in preference to light' and are, in Arnold's view, simply perverse.

Arnold identified the philistines with the new middle class of industrialists: 'The people who believe most that our greatness and welfare are proved by our being very rich, and who most give their lives and thoughts to becoming rich are just the very people whom we call Philistines.'[56] He therefore imagined the philistines to be resisting the sweetness of art as a result of their 'bondage to machinery'.[57] The perverse resistance to the aesthetic is explained as an imprisonment in the technology of capitalism; the philistine may desire beauty, but has made himself unable to respond to it. The philistine position of resistance to the aesthetic is accurately conceived by Arnold, but it is imagined only as a kind of straitjacket in which those whose involvement with the aesthetic might damage their other interests are confined. If, however, we consider Arnold's account of the philistine alongside another text defining the role of culture in the mid-nineteenth century, another possible conception of philistinism emerges. In *Ecce Homo*, Nietzsche mistakenly congratulates himself on having established the word 'culture-philistine' (*Bildungsphilister*) in the German language.[58] He had used it frequently in the first of his *Untimely Meditations*, an attack on the theologian David Strauss. The philistine, Nietzsche wrote, is 'the antithesis of a son of the muses, of the artist, of the man of genuine culture',[59] while the culture-philistine is a philistine who denies that he is a philistine—a sort of nineteenth-century counterpart to all the believing atheists of the sixteenth century. According to Nietzsche: 'An unhappy contortion must have taken place in the brain of the cultural philistine, he regards as culture precisely that which negates culture, and since he is accustomed to proceed with consistency he finally acquires a consistent collection of such negations, a system of un-culture . . . he denies, secretes, stops his ears, averts his eyes, he is a negative being even in his hatred and hostility.' The philistine, Nietzsche continues, is 'a hindrance to the strong and creative, a labyrinth for all who doubt and go astray, a swamp to the feet of the weary, a fetter to all who would pursue lofty goals, a poisonous mist to new buds'.[60]

In this intemperate attack on philistinism, Nietzsche rehearses many elements of his critique of Socrates in *The Birth of Tragedy*, published a year earlier, in 1872. The philistine has 'a certain easy complacency, a self-contentment in one's own limitations' that echoes 'Socratism's complacent delight in existence'.[61] Socrates is also the prototype for Strauss's 'shameless philistine optimism',[62] and just as Socrates has 'art-destroying tendencies', so the philistine 'lodges in the works of our great poets and composers like a worm which lives by destroying'.[63] In *The Birth of Tragedy*, the test of whether someone is a 'true aesthetic listener or belongs to the community of the Socratic-critical persons' is the feeling 'with which he accepts miracles represented on the stage'; in the essay on Strauss, the philistine 'hates the genius: for the genius has the justified reputation of performing miracles'.[64]

Read in the light of Nietzsche's subsequent attack on Strauss, *The Birth of Tragedy* emerges as the unrecognised counterpart of

Culture and Anarchy, published just three years earlier. For although they could hardly be more different in tone, the central concern of the two books is the same. In both *The Birth of Tragedy* and *Culture and Anarchy*, the dichotomy between ordinary and higher experience is accompanied by the suggestion that the higher justifies and gives meaning to the ordinary. Without the elevated, harmonious, and perfected view of the world available through art and culture, the everyday reality experienced by the ordinary self is 'multitudinous, turbulent, and blind' according to Arnold; a nauseating world of pain and contradiction, according to Nietzsche. For Arnold, the only perfect freedom is 'an elevation of our best self, and a harmonizing in subordination to this, and to a perfected humanity, all the . . . impulses of our ordinary selves'.[65] For Nietzsche, 'it is only as an aesthetic phenomenon that the existence and the world are eternally justified', and it is 'the perfection of these states in contrast to the incompletely intelligible everyday world . . . which make life possible and worth living'.[66]

In *The Birth of Tragedy*, the contrast between ordinary and higher experience is articulated through two oppositions: that between Apollo and Silenus, and that between Dionysus and Socrates. According to Nietzsche, the former dichotomy was expressed in Raphael's *Transfiguration*. In the upper half of the picture 'the Apollonian world of beauty', 'a radiant floating in purest bliss, a serene contemplation from wide open eyes'; in the lower the terrible world of Silenus, 'the reflection of suffering primal and eternal'.[67] To illustrate what the world would be like without the redeeming power of the Apollonian, Nietzsche recounted a story told by Sophocles in *Oedipus at Colonus*. Silenus was hunted by Midas and asked, 'What is the best and most desirable of all things for man?' He replies: 'What is best of all is utterly beyond your reach: not to be born, not to be, to be nothing. But the second best for you is—to die soon.' This terrible wisdom was, Nietzsche argued, 'overcome by the Greeks with the aid of the

Olympian middle world of art'.[68] Art 'alone knows how to turn these nauseous thoughts about the horror or absurdity of existence into notions with which one can live'.[69]

Like the Apollonian, the Dionysian is a redemptive art, but one that offers redemption through participation rather than contemplation. According to Nietzsche, 'we have our highest dignity in our significance as works of art', and when in Dionysian 'song and in dance man expresses himself as a member of a higher community. . . . he has become a work of art'.[70] But in Socrates, in whose Cyclops eye 'the fair frenzy of artistic enthusiasm had never glowed',[71] Nietzsche recognised 'the opponent of Dionysus'. Armed with the maxims 'virtue is knowledge; man sins only from ignorance; he who is virtuous is happy', Socrates rejected instinct, and with it the Dionysian element in art.

Taken together, the oppositions between Apollo and Silenus and Dionysus and Socrates form a semiotic square.[72] For while the oppositions between Apollo and Silenus and Dionysus and Socrates are relations of contradictories, the famous Nietzschean distinction between Apollo and Dionysus, and the implied distinction between Silenus and Socrates, are both relations of contraries. Although Nietzsche does not draw attention to it in *The Birth of Tragedy*, the physical similarity between Socrates and Silenus was a commonplace.[73] Between them, they are the twin spokesmen of a world unredeemed by art. The difference between them is best expressed by their attitudes to death. According to Silenus, death is to be preferred to life because life is nothing but suffering; Socrates, having rejected the life-affirming redemption available in art, also prefers death, but only because 'knowledge and reason have liberated [him] from the fear of death'.[74] Thus while Silenus expresses a pre-aesthetic nihilism, Socrates is the exponent of a philistine moralism. Just as Silenus is the anaesthetic expression of the Dionysian, so Socrates, in whom 'the Apollonian tendency has withdrawn into the cocoon of logical schematism',[75] is the anaesthetic counterpart of the redemptive art of Apollo.

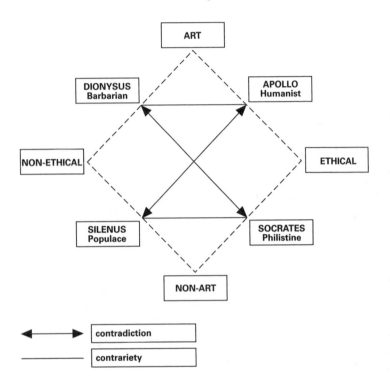

The realization that *The Birth of Tragedy* offers a four-cornered mapping of art and its alternatives allows us to perceive more clearly its affinities with Arnold's categories in *Culture and Anarchy*. Although their evaluation of each alternative is by no means identical, Arnold and Nietzsche articulate the range of positions in congruent terms. In both cases, the distinctions offered are between two forms of culture (the Dionysian and the Apollonian; the barbarian and the humanist) and two forms of non-culture (Silenus and Socrates; the populace and the philistine), and on the other axis between two forms of ethical life (the Apollonian and the Socratic; the humanist and the philistine) and two forms of the non-ethical (the Dionysian and the Silenian; the barbarian and the populace). On this classification, Silenus and the populace remain outside any recognizable culture; the barbarians taste the primitive sweetness of Dionysus; the humanists bathe in the glow of Apollonian light; and Socrates and the philistines perversely resist all the sweetness and light that culture offers. In the delineation of the spectre of philistinism there is therefore striking agreement. The philistine is not merely the spokesperson for one type of culture against another, nor someone for whom culture remains essentially alien, but someone who actively negates the very culture whose benefits they might be expected to share and appreciate. However, in ascribing a motivation to the philistine position, Nietzsche is able to conceive of a more alarming possibility than Arnold can contemplate. To clarify the distinction, it is useful to examine a text that reinterprets *The Birth of Tragedy* in Arnoldian terms—Adorno and Horkheimer's *Dialectic of Enlightenment*.

Odysseus or Socrates?

Despite Habermas's analysis of the Nietzschean undertow in *Dialectic of Enlightenment*,[76] the echoes of *The Birth of Tragedy* in Adorno and Horkheimer's discussion of Odysseus and the Sirens remain obscured. In the first section of *The Birth*, Nietzsche quotes Schopenhauer's image of 'the individual human being . . . supported by and trusting in the *principium individuationis*' as being like a sailor sitting in his frail boat 'in a stormy sea that, unbounded in all directions, raises and drops mountainous waves, howling'.[77] For Adorno and Horkheimer, that sailor is personified by Odysseus, whose adventures have confirmed for him 'the unity of his own life, the identity of the individual',[78] while the Sirens represent one of the 'powers of disintegration' which lure the individual back to the 'womb' of 'prehistoric myth'. Since, according to Nietzsche, 'it is only through the spirit of music that we can understand the joy involved in the annihilation of the individual',[79] it is easy to detect in the Sirens' song the music of Dionysus, which 'does not heed the single unit, but even seeks to destroy the individual and redeem him in a mystic feeling of oneness'.[80] In their invitation to subject the self to nature, the Sirens

rehearse what Nietzsche terms the Dionysian cry of nature: 'Be as I
am. Amid the ceaseless flux of phenomena I am the eternally creative
primordial mother, eternally impelling to existence, eternally finding
satisfaction in the change of phenomena.'[81]

Odysseus, in 'dread of losing the self',[82] plugs the ears of his
sailors with wax and has them bind him with ropes to the mast of
his ship. Although enraptured by the intoxicating sweetness of the
Sirens' song, he is unable to respond to it. Thus, according to
Adorno and Horkheimer, the song of the Sirens 'is neutralised and
becomes a mere object of contemplation—becomes art'.[83] As the
temptations of a participatory and self-annihilatory response are
resisted, so the Dionysian music of the Sirens is transformed into
an Apollonian object of individual appreciation, a harmless
concert. In this way, as Adorno and Horkheimer put it, 'Apollonian
Homer' forges a link between art and individuation.[84]

If Adorno and Horkheimer's interpretation of the Sirens is read
as a reworking of *The Birth of Tragedy*, it soon becomes clear that
Odysseus' resistance to the Sirens is the counterpart of Socrates'
rejection of the Dionysian. Nietzsche himself sets up the parallel in
The Gay Science, where having 'wax in one's ears' is said to have
become a condition of philosophizing because, after Plato, 'a real
philosopher no longer listened to life insofar as life is music', fear-
ing that 'all music is sirens' music'.[85] The philosopher is here placed
in the position of the oarsmen, who are not deaf to the beauty of
the Sirens' music but deaf to the music itself. Odysseus, however,
remains sensible to the beauty of the Sirens' song, yet can only act
as though insensible to it. What he forces himself to resist is the
aesthetic itself; he is literally tied to a philistine position.[86]

For Adorno and Horkheimer, Odysseus is the prototype of the
capitalist who simultaneously deprives his employees of the promise of well-being that the aesthetic invariably offers while at the
same time forcing himself to remain indifferent in order to maintain the efficiency of his enterprise. But the ropes that bind
Odysseus to the mast and so allow him to dominate nature also

imprison him within a purely mechanical worldview: according to Adorno and Horkheimer, 'machinery disables men even as it nurtures them'.[87] This is a profoundly Arnoldian conception of the philistine. Just as Odysseus was bound to the mast of his ship, so Arnold's Victorian philistines were in 'bondage to machinery',[88] tied to the belief that the generation of wealth was an end in itself; the humanists might 'disentangle themselves from machinery', but the philistines cannot escape their preoccupation with 'industrial machinery, and power and pre-eminence'.[89]

By using the Arnoldian image of the philistine externally constrained by ties of his own making, Adorno and Horkheimer are able to remould the Nietzschean narrative of *The Birth of Tragedy* around the story of Odysseus. But in doing so, they lose one essential Nietzschean insight. For Nietzsche, external constraint is a consequence of philistinism and not its cause. In contrast to Odysseus, Socrates is a philistine whose power of resistance comes from within: 'While in all productive men it is instinct that is the creative-affirmative force . . . in Socrates it is instinct that becomes the critic.' When his *daimonion* speaks, it always dissuades: 'in this utterly abnormal nature, instinctive wisdom appears only in order to hinder conscious knowledge'.[90] Even if his followers eventually become 'chained by the Socratic love of knowledge',[91] Socrates himself is not tied to the machinery of domination, but someone through whom the spirit of negation speaks as freely and spontaneously as it does through Silenus. He is not prevented from responding to the music of Dionysus, but liberated from the impulse to do so.

Of course, Nietzsche no sooner creates this philistine monster than he seeks to tame it. Socrates may have rejected art, but Socratism's insatiable quest for knowledge 'speeds irresistibly toward its limits where its optimism, concealed in the essence of logic, suffers shipwreck'.[92] The wisdom of Socrates leads inexorably back to that of his look-alike, Silenus. Redemption is then to be glimpsed in the utopian figure of a Socrates who practises music, an Odysseus who can safely sing along with the Sirens. Yet for all his protests that philistinism will recreate the need for art, Nietzsche, unlike Adorno and Horkheimer, never confuses unfulfilled desire for art with the absence of desire for art. For Nietzsche, the lack of desire for art is a destructive force that eventually reproduces the conditions in which art first became necessary, and although he then hopes for another aesthetic redemption, there is no sense in which the destruction of art itself constitutes or even calls for that redemption. In Socrates, philistinism takes the form of direct and spontaneous negation; unlike Odysseus, he offers a model for what Nietzsche once sarcastically but perhaps prophetically termed 'the philistine as the founder of the religion of the future'.[93]

The Ecstasy of Philistinism

To update Bayle's question, would a society of philistines be possible? Although philistinism may still be invisible, its historical position as the most recent in a sequence of spectral negations suggests that it is not so much unrealizable as temporarily disembodied. In what form might it appear?

Bayle's response to those who doubted the feasibility of a society of atheists was to show how the political and moral values necessary for social order might be furnished by man-made values such as honour or custom as easily as by divine law. In a similar way, Nietzsche describes how a society of nihilists might operate beyond the constraints of morality, while still generating the one surviving form of value—the aesthetic. In both cases, the acceptance of the negation involved an acceptance that the values in question are the product of a particular population organised in a particular way, that value is ultimately a matter of demography and sociology, even biology. If, as Nietzsche claims, 'answers to the question about the *value* of existence may always be considered first of all as the symptoms of certain bodies',[94] then they will always involve 'translating man back into nature', describing him as he now is with intrepid Oedipus eyes and sealed Odysseus ears, deaf to the siren songs of old metaphysical bird catchers who have been piping at him all too long, 'you are more, you are higher, you are of a different origin'.[95]

It is a project Nietzsche shares with Marx, and the *locus classicus* for the conception of society where man has been translated back into nature can be found in Marx's *Economic and Philosophical Manuscripts* of 1844. There Marx envisages communism as 'the complete restoration of man to himself as a *social*, i.e. human, being', which in recognising that 'the *human* essence of nature exists only for *social* man' represents 'the *genuine* resolution of the conflict between man and nature'.[96]

In the restoration of man's social being, all those things that are merely the products of alienation are eliminated. For this reason, Marx claims for communism a privileged and terminal position in the history of negation. Communism represents the positive in the form of 'the negation of the negation'.[97] In economic terms this meant that capitalist private property was 'the first negation of individual private property', and communism's negation of capitalist private property the negation of the negation.[98] Since atheism's negation of religion was seen to be analogous to the communist negation of private property,[99] it too was the negation of a negation. And by this measure, not only atheism, but also anarchism, and nihilism, qualify as negations of a negation, with the result that communism can be seen to embody the sum of all the negations of the negation: 'Religion, the family, the state, law, morality, science, art, etc., are only *particular* modes of production and therefore come under its general law. The positive supersession of *private property*, as the appropriation of *human* life, is therefore the positive supersession of all estrangement, and the return of man from religion, the family, the state, etc., to his *human*, i.e. *social* existence.'[100]

However, the argument has never been extended to include

philistinism, and in consequence the arts have long enjoyed a privileged position in Marxist theory. Marx and Engels envisaged that
'with a communist organization of society, there disappears the
subordination of the artist to local and national narrowness . . . and
also the subordination of the artist to some definite art', but not the
dissolution of the artistic activity. Priest and politician may disappear, but the amateur creative artist remains, along with his
counterpart, the after-dinner critic.[101] No more than Nietzsche,
whose Odysseus has ears sealed to every other siren song of value
save that of art, does Marx consider that the aesthetic might be
anything other than an ineradicable part of the social being of
humanity. Indeed, it is in 'producing according to the laws of
beauty' that man demonstrates his species being in contradistinc-
tion to that of animals.[102]

From this perspective, philistinism is viewed not as a form of
dealienation, but rather as a dehumanization of man which the
return to species being will eventually overcome. In a letter to
Ruge, Marx contrasts human beings, 'that means men of intellect,
free men—that means republicans', with German philistines who,
like animals, only wish 'to live and to procreate'.[103] This is precisely
the condition of alienated labour in which man 'feels that he is
acting freely only in his animal functions . . . while in his human
functions he is nothing more than an animal'.[104] Hence 'the philistine world is the animal kingdom of politics',[105] which communism,
as the restoration of species being to the human world, will inevitably bring to an end.

So, whereas in other spheres the negation of the negation
involved the disappearance of the first negation, in the case of the
arts, the negation of the negation somehow remained an internal
matter, merely requiring the negation of one type of artistic activity by another. In consequence, within the Marxist tradition it has
often been argued that art as such is not a practice that is in its
entirety subject to the dialectic but one through which the dialectic
works. For Adorno, it is precisely this quality of the aesthetic that

is its distinguishing quality. Using the implicitly Nietzschean opposition between (Dionysian) Greek tragedy and the (Apollonian) Greek pantheon to illustrate the point, Adorno argues that the dialectical contradictions within art are the defining characteristic of its utopian promise: 'The unity of art history is captured by the dialectical notion of determinate negation. It is only in this way that art can fulfil its promise of reconciliation.'[106] In Adorno's thought, art is, as Eagleton puts it, 'contradiction incarnate'.[107]

Although Nietzsche imagines that the philistine destruction of art will eventually recreate the need for art, philistinism does not function as merely the negative expression of a new form of art. On the contrary, the Nietzschean figure of Socrates offers a clear picture of the nature and impact of philistinism as a negation that operates not from within the dialectic of art but from without. On this model, even if art is viewed as 'contradiction incarnate', philistinism stands outside it as a form of ecstatic contradiction. Art is not then assimilated to philistinism but annihilated by it, and although the resulting void may yet contain some positive value, that value need not be aesthetic.

Socrates provides the missing model for a philistine negation of the aesthetic negation of humanity's social being—a negation that does not perpetuate art's interminable negation of itself but takes the dialectic beyond art altogether. Socrates is directly opposed to the Dionysian art of tragedy. His was 'the murderous principle' which seeks to destroy 'the essence of tragedy',[108] and although it inspired the Euripidean attempt to write an Apollonian drama, this did not lead to the renewal of tragedy. Dionysian art cannot be assimilated to Socratic philistinism: having abandoned Dionysus, Euripides is abandoned by Apollo, and tragedy dies 'by suicide, in consequence of an irreconcilable conflict'. And when it is dead, there arises 'the deep sense of an immense void. Just as Greek sailors in the time of Tiberius once heard on a lonesome island the soul-shaking cry "Great Pan is dead", so the Hellenistic world was now pierced by the grievous lament: "Tragedy is dead".'[109]

The Open

Socrates, sensing the void, begins to practise music. There is another possibility. Following in the footsteps of Socrates, Nietzsche's madman runs through the marketplace proclaiming the death of God. Astonished by what has happened, he asks, 'How could we drink up the sea? Who gave us the sponge to wipe away the entire horizon?'[110] The void becomes the open. With the news that the old god is dead, it is as if a new day has dawned: 'at long last our ships may venture out again, venture out to face any danger; all the daring of the lover of knowledge is permitted again; the sea, *our* sea, lies open again; perhaps there has never yet been such an "open sea".'[111] Might the disappearance of art also be the opening of a new horizon? Could something as inherently unpromising as philistinism be an opening to anything at all? And if so, where are philistinism's new seas?

Nietzsche here seems to echo Odysseus' words in Dante's *Inferno* when, leaving Ithaca once more, he sets forth 'on the high open sea', urging his crew to take the ship out beyond the pillars of Hercules: 'Consider the seed from which you come / You were not made to live like brutes / But to follow virtue and knowledge'.[112] For the philistine the open lies elsewhere. Rather than the Socrates who practises music, philistinism leaves us with the Socrates in whose eye artistic enthusiasm has never glowed, Socrates as Silenus, half-man and half-animal. To become philistine is, as Marx suggests, to enter 'the animal kingdom of politics'. There, as Rilke has it in the *Duino Elegies*:

> With all eyes the creature sees
> the open. Only our eyes are
> reversed and placed wholly around creatures
> as traps, around their free exit.
> What *is* outside we know from the animal's
> Visage alone . . .[113]

2

Anti-Nietzsche

Many are called, but few are chosen.

Gospel of Matthew

Opposed to everyone, Nietzsche has met with remarkably little opposition. In fact, his reputation has suffered only one apparent reverse—his enthusiastic adoption by the Nazis. But, save in Germany, Nietzsche's association with the horrors of the Second World War and the Holocaust has served chiefly to stimulate further curiosity. Of course, the monster has had to be tamed, and Nietzsche's thought has been cleverly reconstructed so as perpetually to evade the evils perpetrated in his name. Even those philosophies for which he consistently reserved his most biting contempt—socialism, feminism and Christianity—have sought to appropriate their tormentor. Almost everybody now claims Nietzsche as one of their own; he has become what he most wanted to be—irresistible.

This situation gives added significance to a number of recent publications in which the authors reverse the standard practice and straightforwardly report what Nietzsche wrote in order to distance themselves from it. The anti-Nietzschean turn began in France, where Luc Ferry and Alain Renant's collection, *Pourquoi nous ne sommes pas nietzschéens* (1991), responded to the Nietzsche/Marx/Freud syntheses of the preceding decades with the demand that 'We have to stop *interpreting* Nietzsche and start taking him at his word.'[1] The contributors emphasised Nietzsche's opposition to truth and rational argument, the disturbing consequences of his inegalitarianism and immoralism, and his influence on reactionary thought.

Ferry and Renant were seeking to renew a traditional human-ism, but anti-Nietzscheanism can take very different forms. Geoff Waite's cornucopian *Nietzsche's Corps/e* (1996) links the end of Communism and the triumph of Nietzscheanism, and approaches Nietzsche and his body of interpreters from an Althusserian perspective from which Nietzsche emerges as 'the revolutionary programmer of late pseudoleftist, fascoid-liberal culture and tech-noculture'.[2] Claiming that it is now 'blasphemy only to blaspheme *Nietzsche*—formerly the great blasphemer—and *his* community', Waite proceeds to uncover Nietzsche's 'esoteric' teachings, which aim 'to re/produce a viable form of willing human slavery appro-priate to post/modern conditions, and with it a small number of (male) geniuses equal only among themselves'.[3] Integral to this teaching is what Waite calls the '"hermeneutic" or "rhetoric of euthanasia": *the process of weeding out*'. Those who cannot with-stand the thought of Eternal Recurrence are, Nietzsche claims, unfit for life: 'Whosoever will be destroyed with the sentence "there is no salvation" ought to die. I want *wars*, in which the vital and courageous *drive out* the others.'[4]

Although Fredrick Appel's succinctly argued *Nietzsche Contra Democracy* (1999) could hardly be more different from *Nietzsche's Corps/e* in style, the argument is similar. Appel complains that as 'efforts to draft Nietzsche's thought into the service of radical democracy have multiplied his patently inegalitarian political project [has been] ignored or summarily dismissed'. Far from being a protean thinker whose thought is so multifaceted as to resist any single political interpretation, Nietzsche is committed to 'an uncompromising repudiation of both the ethic of benevolence and the notion of the equality of persons in the name of a radically aristocratic commitment to human excellence'.[5] Unlike Waite, who suggests that Nietzsche to some degree concealed his political agenda, Appel argues that it pervades every aspect of Nietzsche's later thought. Nietzsche's elitism is not only fundamental to his entire worldview, it is so profound that it leads naturally to the conclusion that 'the great majority of men have no right to existence'.[6]

In fact, as Domenico Losurdo demonstrates in his monumental contextual study, *Nietzsche, il ribelle aristocratico* (2002), Nietzsche's political agenda was not confined to his later thought. From the start, Nietzsche's work embodies a direct response to contemporary political developments continuous with that of other reactionaries. Written in the aftermath of the Franco-Prussian war, *The Birth of Tragedy* could easily have been subtitled *The Crisis of Culture from Socrates to the Paris Commune*, for Socrates embodies the deracinated rationalism and optimism, Hebrew in origin but now French in expression, that threatens the 'tragic vision of the world' of the early Greeks and modern Germans. Far from being metaphorical, Nietzsche's politics is eminently practical. His plan for new forms of slavery is a response to its recent abolition in the United States, and includes realistic suggestions for its implementation. His idealisation of war echoes European perceptions of colonial conquest, and the assumption that weaker individuals and races will be exterminated in such wars reflects contemporary realities. Nietzsche does not hesitate to give examples of what he has in mind: his model of racial dominance is the Congo; his vision of a 'great politics' is premised on a European invasion of Russia.[7]

Nevertheless, Nietzsche's affinity with Nazism is with its means more than its ends. As some of the contributors to *Nietzsche, Godfather of Fascism?* (2002) point out, being largely opposed to German nationalism, anti-Semitism, and the power of the state, Nietzsche could not have been an uncritical Nazi.[8] But his reservations would not necessarily have extended to cataclysmic war, mass extermination, the renewal of slavery and the breeding of a master race, since these were all things he contemplated with equanimity. If anything, Nietzsche might have seen Nazism not as a grotesque extrapolation of his ideas, but as one that was too limited—vulgar in expression, parochial in ambition, too petty in its cruelties.

Most people probably would not want to be implicated in a political philosophy of this kind. But is it possible to distance yourself from Nietzsche without having to meet him again? Nietzsche's arguments were explicitly formulated against the practices of social levelling and liberation found within liberalism, socialism and feminism. Most of his recent critics seek to reaffirm political and philosophical positions that Nietzsche himself repudiated. For them, reestablishing that Nietzsche was an amoral, irrationalist, antiegalitarian who had no respect for basic human rights suffices as a means of disposing of his arguments. Yet if opposition comes only from within the preexisting traditions, it will do little to dislodge Nietzsche from the position that he chose for himself— the philosopher of the future who writes 'for a species of man that does not yet exist'.[9]

The self-styled Anti-Christ who placed himself on the last day of Christianity, and at the end of the secular European culture that it had fostered, would not be displeased if his 'revaluation of all values' were to be indefinitely rejected by those who continued to adhere to the values he despised. He would live forever as their eschatological nemesis, the limit-philosopher of a modernity that never ends, waiting to be born posthumously on the day after tomorrow. What seems to be missing is any critique of Nietzsche that takes the same retrospective position that Nietzsche adopted with regard to Christianity. Postmodernity spawned plenty of post-Nietzscheans anxious to appropriate Nietzsche for their own agendas, but there have been few post-Nietzschean anti-Nietzscheans—critics whose response is designed not to prevent us from getting to Nietzsche, but to enable us to get over him.

Reading Nietzsche

The chief impediment to the development of any form of anti-Nietzscheanism is, as Waite points out, that 'most readers basically *trust* him'.[10] One reason for this is that Nietzsche gives readers strong incentives to do so. 'This book belongs to the very few', he announces in the foreword to *The Anti-Christ*. It belongs only to those who are 'honest in intellectual matters to the point of harshness'; who have 'strength which prefers questions for which no one today is sufficiently daring; courage for the *forbidden*':

> These alone are my readers, my rightful readers, my predestined readers: what do the *rest* matter?—The rest are merely mankind.— One must be superior to mankind in force, in *loftiness* of soul—in contempt.[11]

Through the act of reading, Nietzsche flatteringly offers identification with the masters to anyone, but not to everyone. Identification with the masters means imaginative liberation from all the social, moral and economic constraints within which individuals are usually confined; identification with 'the rest' involves reading one's way through many pages of abuse directed at people like oneself. Unsurprisingly, people of all political persuasions and social positions have more readily discovered themselves to belong to the former category. For who, in the privacy of reading, can fail to find within themselves some of those qualities of honesty and courage and loftiness of soul that Nietzsche describes?

As Wyndham Lewis observed, there is an element of fairground trickery in this strategy: 'Nietzsche, got up to represent a Polish nobleman, with a *berserker* wildness in his eye, advertised the secrets of the world, and sold little vials containing blue ink, which he represented as drops of authentic blue blood, to the delighted populace. They went away, swallowed his prescriptions, and felt very noble almost at once.'[12] Put like this, it sounds as though

Nietzsche's readers are simply credulous. But there is more to it. Take Stanley Rosen's account of the same phenomenon in Nietzsche's reception: 'An appeal to the highest, most gifted human individuals to create a radically new society of artist-warriors was expressed with rhetorical power and a unique mixture of frankness and ambiguity in such a way as to allow the mediocre, the foolish, and the mad to regard themselves as the divine prototypes of the highest men of the future.'[13] How many of those who read this statement regard themselves as these 'divine prototypes'? Very few, I suspect. For in uncovering Nietzsche's rhetorical strategy Rosen reuses it. The juxtaposition of 'the highest, most gifted human individuals' to whom Nietzsche addressed himself, and 'the mediocre, the foolish, and the mad' who claimed what was not rightfully theirs, encourages readers to distance themselves from the former category and identify with the 'gifted human individuals' who, it is implied, passed up the opportunity that Nietzsche offered. Like Lewis, Rosen invites his readers to consider the possibility that Nietzsche is only for the little people, and that being a mere Superman[14] may well be beneath them.

Nietzsche's strategy is one from which it is difficult for readers wholly to disentangle themselves. And in *Nietzsche's Dangerous Game*, Daniel Conway argues that it is just this strategy that is central to Nietzsche's post-Zarathustra philosophy. Isolated, and seemingly ignored, the late Nietzsche desperately needs readers, for otherwise his grandiose claims about the epochal significance of his own philosophy cannot possibly be justified. But insofar as his readers passively accept his critique of earlier philosophy, they will hardly be the 'monsters of courage and curiosity' needed to transmit his philosophy to the future. However, if Nietzsche's readers actually embody those adventurous qualities he idealises, they will quickly detect 'his own complicity in the decadence of modernity'.[15] Paradoxically, therefore, Nietzscheanism is best preserved through readings which expose Nietzsche's decadence and so make him the first martyr to his own strategy. Indeed,

Conway's own practice of 'reading Nietzsche against Nietzsche' is, as he acknowledges, one example, and so, according to his own argument, ironically serves to perpetuate a Nietzscheanism without Nietzsche: 'the apostasy of his children is never complete. They may turn on him, denounce him, even profane his teachings, but they do so only by implementing the insights and strategies he has bequeathed to them.'[16] As a result, one aspect of Nietzsche's programme, his suspicion, is forever enacted against another, his critique of decadence, for the suspicion that unmasks the decadence even of the 'master of suspicion' is itself a symptom of decadence waiting to be unmasked by future generations, themselves schooled in suspicion by their own decadence.

Although Conway illustrates ways in which both Nietzsche and his 'signature doctrines' are potentially the victims of his own strategy, he does little to show how the reader can avoid participating in it. In fact, Conway appears to be deploying a more sophisticated version of the Nietzschean response used by Lewis and Rosen. Rather than simply inviting readers to think of themselves as being superior to the foolish mediocrities who would be Supermen, Conway encourages the reader to join him in the higher task of unmasking the Supermen, and Nietzsche himself. But is there no way to reject Nietzsche without at the same time demonstrating one's masterly superiority to the herd of slavish Nietzscheans from whom one is distinguishing oneself? Can the reader resist, or at least fail to follow, Nietzsche's injunction: 'one must be superior'?

Reading for Victory

The act of reading always engages the emotions of readers, and to a large degree the success of any text (or act of reading) depends upon a reader's sympathetic involvement. A significant part of that involvement comes from the reader's identification with individuals or types within the story. People routinely identify with the heroes of narratives, and with almost any character who is presented in an attractive light. This involves 'adopting the goals of a protagonist' to the extent that the success or failure of those goals occasions an emotional response in the reader similar to that which might be expected of the protagonist, irrespective of whether the protagonist is actually described as experiencing those emotions.[17] Hence, a story with a happy ending is one in which the reader feels happy because of the hero's success, and a sad story is one in which the protagonist is unsuccessful.

Within this process, readers sometimes identify with the goals of characters who may be in many or all external respects (age, race, gender, class, etc.) dissimilar to themselves. But the goals with which they identify—escaping death, finding a mate, achieving personal fulfilment—are almost always ones shared by the reader in that they reflect rational self-interest. The effect of identifying with the goals of protagonists on the basis of self-interest is that the act of reading becomes an attempt to succeed in the same objectives that the reader pursues in everyday life. Indeed, success in the act of reading may actually serve to compensate readers for their relative inability to realise those same objectives in their own lives. Hence perhaps the apparent paradox generated by Nietzsche's popularity among disadvantaged groups he went out of his way to denigrate. They, too, are reading for victory, struggling to wrest success from the text by making themselves the heroes of Nietzsche's narrative.

Reading for victory is the way Nietzsche himself thought people ought to read. As he noted in *Human, All Too Human*:

> He who really wants to get to *know* something new (be it a person, an event, a book) does well to entertain it with all possible love and to avert his eyes quickly from everything in it he finds inimical . . . so that, for example, he allows the author of a book the longest start, and then, like one watching a race, desires with beating heart that he may reach his goal.[18]

When he wrote this, Nietzsche considered that reading for victory was only a device and that reason might eventually catch up. But in his later writings, this possibility is dismissed. Knowledge 'works as a tool of power' and so 'increases with every increase of power'.[19] The reader's yearning for victory is now not a means to knowledge but an example of what knowledge is. Getting to know something is no more than the act of interpreting it to one's own advantage: 'The will to power *interprets* . . . In fact, interpretation is itself a means of becoming master of something.'[20]

In this context, reading for victory without regard to the objections or consequences of that reading is more than reading the way we usually read: it is also our first intoxicating taste of the will to power. Not only does reading for victory exemplify the will to power, but in reading Nietzsche our exercise of the will to power is actually rewarded with the experience of power. It is possible to see this happen even in a single sentence. Take Nietzsche's boast in *Ecce Homo*, 'I am not a man, I am dynamite.'[21] Reading these words, who has not felt the sudden thrill of something explosive within themselves; or, at the very least, emboldened by Nietzsche's daring, allowed themselves to feel a little more expansive than usual? This, after all, is the way we usually read. Even though Nietzsche is attributing the explosive power to himself, not to us, we instantly appropriate it for ourselves.

Here perhaps is the root of Nietzsche's extraordinary bond with his readers. Reading Nietzsche successfully means reading for victory, reading so that we identify ourselves with the goals of the author. In so unscrupulously seeking for ourselves the rewards of the text we become exemplars of the uninhibited will to power. No wonder Nietzsche can so confidently identify his readers with the Supermen. It is not just flattery. If Nietzsche's readers have mastered his text, they have demonstrated just those qualities of ruthlessness and ambition that qualify them to be 'masters of the earth'. But they have done more than earn a status in Nietzsche's fictional world. In arriving at an understanding of

Nietzsche's cardinal doctrine they have already proved it to themselves. Nietzsche persuades by appealing to experience—not to our experience of the world, but our experience as readers, in particular, our experience as readers of his text.

Reading like a Loser

There is an alternative to reading for victory: reading like a loser. Robert Burton described it and its consequences in *The Anatomy of Melancholy:*

> Yea, but this meditation is that marres all, and mistaken makes many men farre worse, misconceaving all they reade or heare, to their owne overthrow, the more they search and reade Scriptures, or divine Treatises, the more they pussle themselves, as a bird in a net, the more they are intangled and precipitated into this preposterous gulfe. *Many are called, but few are chosen, Mat. 20.16 and 22.14.* With such like places of Scripture misinterpreted strike them with horror, they doubt presently whether they be of this number or no, gods eternall decree of predestination, absolute reprobation, & such fatall tables they forme to their owne ruine, and impinge upon this rocke of despaire.[22]

To read to one's own overthrow is an unusual strategy. It differs equally from the rejection of a text as mistaken or immoral and from the assimilation of a text as compatible with one's own being. Reading like a loser means assimilating a text in such a way that it is incompatible with one's self.

The interpretative challenge presented by the doctrine of predestination is in important respects similar to the one Nietzsche offers his readers. The underlying presupposition of both is that many are called, and few are chosen. One might suppose that the majority of those faced with the doctrine would deduce that they are more likely to be among the many than the few. But, just as almost all of Nietzsche's readers identify themselves as being among the few who are honest, strong and courageous, so generations of Christians have discovered themselves to be among the few who are 'called'. The alternative, although seemingly logical, was so rare as to be considered pathological. People were not expected to survive in this state. As Burton noted: 'Never was any living creature in such torment . . . in such miserable estate, in such distresse of minde, no hope, no faith, past cure, reprobate, continually tempted to make away with themselves.'[23]

Reading like losers, we respond very differently to the claims Nietzsche makes on behalf of himself and his readers. Rather than reading for victory with Nietzsche, or even reading for victory against Nietzsche by identifying with the slave morality, we read for victory against ourselves, making ourselves the victims of the text. Doing so does not involve treating the text with scepticism or suspicion. In order to read like a loser you have to accept the argument, but turn its consequences against yourself. So, rather than thinking of ourselves as dynamite, or questioning Nietzsche's extravagant claim, we will immediately think (as we might if someone said this to us in real life) that there may be an explosion; that we might get hurt; that we are too close to someone who could harm us. Reading like losers will make us feel powerless and vulnerable.

The net result, of course, is that reading Nietzsche will become far less pleasurable. When we read that 'Those who are from the outset victims, downtrodden, broken—they are the ones, the *weakest* are the ones who most undermine life',[24] we will think primarily of ourselves. Rather than being an exhilarating vision of the limitless possibilities of human emancipation, Nietzsche's texts will continually remind us of our own weakness and mediocrity, and our irremediable exclusion from the life of joy and careless laughter that is possible only for those who are healthier and more powerful. In consequence, we will never experience the mysterious alchemy of Nietzsche's texts in which the reader reaps the benefits of Nietzsche's doctrine in the act of apprehending it.

How then will we feel about Nietzsche? We might answer the way Nietzsche suggests no one has ever answered: ' "I don't like him."— Why?—"I am not equal to him." '[25] In any case, we will not be able to look him in the face as he asks us to do.[26] His gaze is too piercing, his presence too powerful. We must lower our eyes and turn away.

The Philistine

Reading Nietzsche like losers is likely to prove more difficult than we might suppose. It involves more than distancing ourselves from his more extravagant claims; it means that we will find it impossible to identify with any of his positive values. This may prove painful, for some of Nietzsche's values are widely endorsed within contemporary culture, and accepting our inability to share them may count as an intellectual and social failing. This is perhaps most obviously true when it comes to art, the one thing to which Nietzsche consistently ascribed a positive value.

It was in *The Birth of Tragedy* that Nietzsche first articulated the view that life was meaningless and unbearable, and that 'it is only as an *aesthetic phenomenon* that existence and the world are eternally *justified*'.[27] Although he subsequently distanced himself from this early work, Nietzsche never gave up the idea that art was the one redemptive value in the world, or that 'we have our highest dignity in our significance as works of art'.[28] In his later writings, the role of art comes to be identified with the will to power. As Nietzsche noted in a draft for the new preface to *The Birth of Tragedy:*

> Art and nothing but art! It is the great means of making life possible, the great seduction to life, the great stimulant of life.
>
> Art as the only superior counterforce to all will to denial of life, as that which is anti-Christian, anti-Buddhist, antinihilist *par excellence*.[29]

Whereas other putative sources of value, such as religion and morality and philosophical truth, placed themselves in opposition to life, art was not something that stood over and against life, it was the affirmation of life, and so also life's affirmation of itself.

Nietzsche's later vision of art as the value that supersedes all others has two related elements: the role of the aesthetic as a source of value, and the artist as a creator and embodiment of that value. But if we are reading like losers, we are not going to be able to identify with either of these things. We will think of ourselves as philistines who are unable to appreciate what is supposedly the aesthetic dimension of experience; as people who have no taste or discrimination, no capacity to appreciate what are meant to be the finer things of life. This does not just involve distancing ourselves from the rarefied discourse of traditional aesthetics; it means not being able to see the point of avant-gardist repudiations of tradition either.

According to Nietzsche, 'the effect of works of art is to *excite the state that creates art*'. Being an aesthete is therefore indistinguishable from being an artist, for 'All art . . . speaks only to artists.'[30] Reading like losers places us outside this equation: unable to appreciate, we are also unable to create. We cannot think of ourselves as original or creative people, only as creatures, the material that must be 'formed, broken, forged, torn, burnt . . . and purified'.[31] When we read Nietzsche's descriptions of the 'inartistic state' that subsists 'among those who become impoverished, withdraw, grow pale, under whose eyes life suffers',[32] we should not hurry to exclude ourselves. In Nietzsche's opinion, '*the aesthetic state* . . . appears only in natures capable of that bestowing and overflowing fullness of bodily vigor . . . [But] the sober, the weary, the exhausted, the dried-up (e.g. scholars) can receive absolutely nothing from art, because they do not possess the primary artistic force.'[33] 'Yes,' the loser responds, 'that sounds like me.'

It may not appear to be a very attractive option, for Nietzsche deliberately makes it as unappealing as possible, but acknowledging a lack of 'the primary artistic force' must be the starting point for any anti-Nietzscheanism. Anyone who does not do so retains an important stake in Nietzsche's vision of the future. Receptivity to the aesthetic is the ticket to privilege in Nietzsche's world; the only people liable to suffer from his revaluation of values are those who lack it. Nietzsche may claim that only a select minority are likely to qualify, but in a culture where self-identified philistines are conspicuous by their absence, it is not surprising to discover that Nietzsche's readers have consistently found themselves to be included rather than excluded from his vision of the future.

The Subhuman

To find the Anti-Nietzsche it is necessary to locate oneself not only outside contemporary culture, but outside the human species altogether. Nietzsche's model for the future of intraspecific relations is based on that of interspecific relations in the natural world. The underlying analogy is that Superman is to man as man is to animal. Zarathustra pictures man as 'a rope stretched between animal and Superman—a rope over an abyss'.[34] The philosopher of the future must walk the tightrope. Unlike those who would rather return to the animal state, the Supermen will establish the same distance between themselves and other humans as humans have established between themselves and animals:

> All creatures hitherto have created something beyond themselves, and do you want to be the ebb of this great tide and return to the animals rather than overcome man?

> What is the ape to men? A laughing stock or a painful embarrassment. And just so shall man be to the Superman: a laughing stock or a painful embarrassment.[35]

Indeed, Nietzsche repeatedly refers to Supermen as being a different species: 'I write for a species of man that does not yet exist: for the "masters of the earth"'.[36] He was not speaking metaphorically, either. He hoped that the new species might be created through selective breeding, and noted the practical possibility of 'international racial unions whose task will be to rear the master race, the future "masters of the earth"'.[37]

According to Nietzsche, it follows from this that, relative to the Supermen, ordinary mortals will have no rights whatsoever. The Supermen have duties only to their equals; 'towards the others one acts as one thinks best'.[38] The argument here is also based on inter-specific analogies. Nietzsche conceives the difference between man and Superman not only in terms of that between animal and man, but on the model of herd animal and predatory animal. He introduced the idea in *The Genealogy of Morals* in a discussion of lambs and birds of prey. Noting that it is hardly strange that lambs bear ill will towards large birds of prey, he argues this is 'in itself no reason to blame large birds of prey for making off with little lambs'. According to Nietzsche,

> To demand of strength that it should *not* express itself as strength, that it should *not* be a will to overcome, overthrow, dominate, a thirst for enemies and resistance and triumph, makes as little sense as to demand of weakness that it should express itself as strength.

The argument hinges on the idea of carnivorousness as an expression of the amorality that is a natural and inescapable feature of interspecific relations. Nietzsche imagines his birds of prey saying '*We* bear them no ill will at all, these good lambs—indeed, we love them; there is nothing tastier than a tender lamb.'[39] However it may appear to the lambs, for the carnivore eating them it is not a question of ethics, just a matter of taste. Nietzsche therefore argues that were a comparable divide to exist between two human species, the Supermen and the herd animals who sustain them, relations between the species would also be entirely governed by the tastes of the superior species. Nietzsche does not say whether the

Supermen will feast upon their human subordinates, but it is inconceivable that he should have any objection to the practice, save perhaps gastronomic.

Nietzsche's analogy relies on the assumption that the patterns of interspecific relations are unquestioned and that it will be easier for the reader to imagine eating other species than it is to imagine being eaten by them. The raptors' response to the lamb is therefore also that of carnivorous readers, who also love lamb as much as they love lambs. Reading like losers, however, we may identify with man rather than Superman, with the animal rather than man, and with the herd animal rather than the predator. The pattern of interspecific behaviour that Nietzsche describes will immediately strike us as terrifying. We could be eaten.

Consistently thinking about the human from the perspective of the subhuman is difficult, but in reading like a loser we have to give up the idea of becoming more than man and think only of becoming something less. Nietzsche himself identified becoming subhuman with the egalitarian projects of democracy and socialism:

> The *over-all degeneration of man* down to what today appears to the socialist dolts and flatheads as their 'man of the future'—as their ideal—this degeneration and diminution of man into the perfect herd animal (or, as they say, to the man of the 'free society'), this animalization of man into the dwarf animal of equal rights and claims, is *possible*, there is no doubt of it.

The prospect strikes Nietzsche with horror: 'Anyone who has once thought through this possibility to the end knows one kind of nausea that other men don't know.'[40] Even those who consider Nietzsche to have offered an absurd caricature of the socialist project would probably agree that the subhumanisation of man was a repulsive goal. But if we are reading like losers we may think differently. Just as the superhumanisation of man will fill us with terror, the dehumanisation of man into a herd animal will strike us as offering a welcome respite from a cruel predator and as opening up new possibilities for subhuman sociality. And although the subhuman, like the philistine, may not seem like the most promising basis for a thoroughgoing anti-Nietzscheanism, it is more than just a hypothetical counter-Nietzschean position generated by a perverse strategy of reading: the subhuman and the philistine are not two forms of the Anti-Nietzsche but one.

Negative Ecology of Value

Nietzsche's project is the revaluation of all values. There are two stages: the first nihilistic, the second ecological. Nietzsche acknowledged himself to be 'a thorough-going nihilist', and although he says he accepted this only in the late 1880s, the idea obviously appealed, for he then proclaimed himself to be 'the first perfect nihilist of Europe'.[41] What Nietzsche means is that he has accepted, more completely than anyone before him, the 'absolute untenability of existence when it comes to the highest values one recognizes'.[42] All the values of religion and morality which were supposed to make life worth living are unsustainable; scepticism has undermined the lot. The truthfulness enjoined by religion and morality has shown the values of religion and morality (including the value of truth itself) to be fictitious. In this way, the highest values of the past have devalued themselves. Nihilism is not something that has worked against religion and morality; it has worked through them. The advent of nihilism, the realisation that everything that was thought to be of value is valueless, therefore represents both the triumph of Christian values and their annihilation. As Heidegger observed, 'for Nietzsche, nihilism is not in any way simply a phenomenon of decay; rather nihilism is, as the fundamental event of Western history, simultaneously and above all the intrinsic law of that history'.[43]

Although Nietzsche does not repudiate nihilism, he anticipates that in the future it will take another form. He argues that 'the universe seems to have lost value, seems "meaningless"—but that is only a *transitional stage*'.[44] What lies beyond it is 'a movement that in some future will take the place of this perfect nihilism—but presupposes it, logically and psychologically'.[45] The movement is the one that Nietzsche describes as the revaluation of all values. The presupposition of this is that 'we require, sometime, *new values*', but not values of the old kind that measure the value of the world in terms of things outside it, for they 'refer to a purely fictitious world'.[46] Nietzsche's revaluation of values demands more than this, 'an overturning of the nature and manner of valuing'.[47]

Nietzsche never uses the word, but the form of this revaluation of valuing is perhaps most accurately described as ecological, not because Nietzsche exhibited any particular concern for the natural environment, but on account of the unprecedented conjunction of two ideas: the recognition of the interdependence of values, and the evaluation of value in biological terms. As a pioneer in the study of the history of values, Nietzsche sought 'knowledge of their growth, development, displacement'.[48] Values did not coexist in an unchanging timeless harmony. Within history some values had displaced others because not all values can simultaneously be equally valuable. Some values negate and devalue others: Christianity had involved 'a revaluation of all the values of antiquity', for the ancient values, 'pride . . . the deification of passion, of revenge, of cunning, of anger, of voluptuousness, of adventure, of knowledge', could not prosper in the new moral climate.[49] And the same could happen again: 'Moral values have hitherto been the highest values: would anybody call this in question?—If we remove these values from this position, we alter all values: the principle of their order of rank hitherto is thus overthrown.'[50] In consequence, the revaluation of values involves not the invention of new values, but reinventing the relationships between the old ones: 'The future task of the philosopher: this task being understood as the solution of the *problem of value*, [is] the determination of the *hierarchy of values*.'[51]

If it was as a genealogist of values that Nietzsche discovered their precarious ecology, it was as a nihilist that he sought to exploit it. Nietzsche recognised that, just as asserting one value negated another, so the denial of value placed a positive valuation upon the negation itself. The one irreducible value was therefore the value of valuation. But since, for a nihilist, values are valueless in themselves, the value of valuation is not merely the last value but the only one. As Nietzsche states, nihilism 'places the value of things precisely in the lack of any reality corresponding to these values and in their being merely a symptom of strength on the part of the value-positers'.[52] The effect of this argument is heavily reductive, for if the only value is valuation, then all that is of value is the capacity to establish values, a capacity that Nietzsche equates with life itself: 'When we speak of values we do so under the inspiration and from the perspective of life: life itself evaluates through us *when* we establish values.'[53] However, life itself is contested, and so 'There is nothing to life that has value except the degree of power—assuming that life itself is the will to power.'[54]

As a historian, Nietzsche noted that 'Values and their changes are related to increases in the power of those positing the values',[55] but, according to his own reductive argument, changes in value are not merely related to changes in power; they are themselves those changes in power, for the value is 'the highest quantum of power that a man is able to incorporate'.[56] So, because value resides in valuation, and valuation exists only where there is the power to establish values, the ecology of value within the realm of ideas becomes a literal biological ecology of living organisms. As Nietzsche puts it:

> The standpoint of 'value' is the standpoint of conditions of preservation and enhancement for complex forms of relative life-duration within the flux of becoming.[57]

In short, value is ultimately ecological, in that what is of value is the conditions that allow valuation. And since, according to

Nietzsche, 'it is the intrinsic right of *masters* to create values',[58] the task of the philosopher is that of defining the ecology in which such valuation is possible. Not being familiar with the twentieth-century concept of the ecologist, Nietzsche imagines a new type of physician whose concern is with the health of society as a whole:

> I am still waiting for a philosophical *physician* in the exceptional sense of that word—one who has to pursue the problem of the total health of a people, time, race or of humanity—to muster the courage to push my suspicion to its limits and to risk the proposition: what was at stake in all philosophizing hitherto was not at all 'truth' but something else—let us say, health, future, growth, power, life.[59]

What this global ecologist of value would do is create conditions that foster the production of value-positers. And since the 'higher type is possible only through the subjugation of the lower',[60] this means breeding a master species capable of enslaving the rest of the world:

> a new, tremendous aristocracy, based on the severest self-legislation, in which the will of philosophical men of power and artist-tyrants will be made to endure for millennia—a higher kind of man who . . . employ democratic Europe as their most pliant and supple instrument for getting hold of the destinies of the earth, so as to work as artists upon 'man' himself.[61]

In this ecology, the philistine and the subhuman are the same thing. Nietzsche equates receptivity to the aesthetic with being an artist, being an artist with the capacity for valuation, and the capacity for valuation with the exercise of power. Just as his artist-tyrants display their artistry through their tyranny and exercise their tyranny in their artistry, so philistinism is the mark of the subhuman, and subhumanisation the fate of the philistine. Because they fail to participate in art, the '*affirmation, blessing, deification,* of existence',[62] philistines lack will to power and are enslaved. And because subhumans lack the power to create value, they can never appreciate it either. Within the ecology of value a certain number of subhuman-philistines are always necessary in order to act as slaves to the supermen-aesthetes, but since an ecology of value is one that fosters the production of supermen-aesthetes rather than subhuman-philistines, it follows that any increase in the latter, beyond the minimum needed to serve the needs of their masters, will have a negative effect on that ecology. Nietzsche's vision of the future naturally includes provision for the extermination of these vermin, for their proliferation will do more than have a negative effect on his ecology of value; since the ecology of value is the last remaining value in the history of nihilism, its negation is the ultimate negation of value itself.

It is worth considering the implications of this a little further. For a thoroughgoing nihilist the last value must be derived from the negation of value. Since valuation is unavoidable, it would seem to follow that valuation is that last value. And this is why Nietzsche thinks that the ecology of value will be the ultimate conclusion of his nihilism. But this is not so. Although value might ultimately be ecological, it does not follow that its ecology is valuable. Rather than a positive ecology of value, which creates the possibility for conditions of valuation, there might be a negative ecology—an ecology that minimises the possibilities for the positing of value and so reduces the quantum of value still further. The full significance of the philistine and the subhuman now becomes clearer. Reading Nietzsche as a philistine-subhuman is not just a matter of finding a perspective from which Nietzsche's ideas appear alien and threatening; it actually constitutes a countermove to Nietzsche's strategy. Reading for victory exemplifies the will to power and promotes an ecology of value by increasing the numbers of those who are value-positers; reading like a loser has a direct negative impact on that ecology since it decreases the proportion of value-positers. Taking up the role of the philistine-subhuman therefore continues the nihilistic dynamic that Nietzsche thought he had ended, not by perpetuating the *ressentiment* of slave morality—reading like a loser is not an affirmation of the values through which losers become winners—but by having a direct, negative impact on the ecology of value.

Total Society

It might appear that a negative ecology of value could feature on only the most perverse of dystopian agendas. But that would be a hasty judgement. The negative ecology of value, which Nietzsche called 'the kingdom of heaven of the poor in spirit', had in his view already begun:

> The French Revolution as the continuation of Christianity. Rousseau is the seducer: he again unfetters woman who is henceforth represented in an ever more interesting manner—as suffering. Then the slaves and Mrs Beecher-Stowe. Then the poor and the workers. Then the vice addicts and the sick . . . We are well on the way: the kingdom of heaven of the poor in spirit has begun.[63]

The way in which this process served to negate value is spelt out most clearly with regard to slavery: ' "Abolition of slavery"— supposedly a tribute to "human dignity", in fact a destruction of a fundamentally different type (—the undermining of its values and happiness—).'[64] Rather than accepting the rhetoric of liberation on its own terms, and seeing it as an extension of the ecology of value which attributes positive qualities to those who are liberated, Nietzsche sees it only as a negation of the values reposed within the masters. Thus, the liberation of women serves only to negate the special value of masculinity; the emancipation of slaves the value of whiteness, the liberation of the workers the value of capital, the liberation of the sick the seemingly unarguable value of health itself.

Those who seek to oppose Nietzsche typically reject his analysis of these changes and maintain that the long process of human emancipation has not only been motivated by the desire to promote values but has also contributed to their ecology. But, as has often been noted, this argument is difficult to sustain at a historical or sociological level. Whatever the intentions of those who have promoted these social reforms, their effect has not been to strengthen value, but rather to dilute it by widening its scope. Durkheim, writing shortly after Nietzsche, was perhaps the first to note the pattern. Laws against murder are now more inclusive than in former times, but

> If all the individuals who . . . make up society are today protected to an equal extent, this greater mildness in morality is due, not to the emergence of a penal rule that is really new, but to the extension of the scope of an ancient rule. From the beginning there was a prohibition on attempts to take the life of any member of the group, but children and slaves were excluded from this category. Now that we no longer make such distinctions actions have become punishable that once were not criminal. But this is merely because there are more persons in society, and not because collective sentiments have increased in number. These have not grown, but the object to which they relate has done so.[65]

Indeed, as he argued in *The Division of Labour in Society*, the *conscience collective*, the set of values shared by a social group, is progressively weakened by increases in the size and complexity of the unit. Taken to its limits, the dynamic that Durkheim describes involves the totalisation of society to its maximal inclusiveness and complexity, and the corresponding elimination of shared values. Already, he suggests, morality 'is in the throes of an appalling crisis'.[66] If the totalisation of society and the weakening of *la conscience collective* is not balanced by the development of organic solidarity through the division of labour, the change will result only in *anomie*.

Although they emphasise different aspects of the process, it is clear that Durkheim and Nietzsche are addressing the same issue. Both describe the origins of morality in the customs of communities bound together by what Durkheim called 'mechanical solidarity'. But what is, for Durkheim, the expansion of the group and the weakening of *la conscience collective,* is, for Nietzsche, the slave revolt in morals and the beginnings of European nihilism:

> Refraining mutually from injury, violence, and exploitation and placing one's will on a par with that of someone else—this may become . . . good manners among individuals if the appropriate conditions are present (namely, if these men are actually similar in strength and value standards and belong together in *one* body). But as soon as this principle is extended, and possibly even accepted as the *fundamental principle of society,* it immediately proves to be what it really is—a will to the *denial* of life, a principle of disintegration and decay.[67]

Durkheim is nervously optimistic about the totalisation of society. Observing that 'there is tending to form, above European peoples, in a spontaneous fashion, a European society', he argued that even if 'the formation of one single human society is forever ruled out— and this has, however, not yet been demonstrated—at least the formation of larger societies will draw us continually closer to that goal'.[68] In contrast, Nietzsche's response is to demand a return to mechanical solidarity, not of course for everyone, but for the few strong men who can create value. Only if society is detotalised and redivided into the community of the strong and the undifferentiated mass of the weak can the conditions for value creation be sustained:

As a good man, one belongs to the 'good', a community that has a sense of belonging together because all the individuals in it are combined with one another through the capacity for requital. As a bad man, one belongs to the 'bad', to a swarm of subject, powerless people who have no sense of belonging together.[69]

In this context, our reading of Nietzsche assumes additional importance. Identifying positively with any narrative (written or otherwise) means making its goals one's own. And although we may not be trying to make common cause with other readers, reading for victory has a strong centripetal dynamic: the greater our success, the more closely our goals converge with those of others who are doing the same thing. Reading Nietzsche for victory is the route to his new mechanical solidarity. In contrast, reading like losers is centrifugal. Since we are not in any sense opposed to the text, we have no common cause even with those who are reading for victory against it; we just become part of that 'mass of abject, powerless men who have no communal feeling'. Reading like a loser, in its consistent exclusion of the reader from shared value, is a willingness to exchange an exclusive communality for an inclusive and indiscriminate sociality.

Becoming part of a mass with no communal feeling may negate the ecology of value, but such a mass is not necessarily a negative ecology. Like Nietzsche, Durkheim thought of society in biological terms. His model of organic solidarity is an oak tree which can sustain 'up to two hundred species of insects that have no contacts with one another save those of good neighbourliness'.[70] Just as an environment can sustain a higher population the greater the diversity of the species within it, so society can accommodate more people if they have less in common and more diversified social roles. But whereas Durkheim's ecology is acknowledged to be part of a negative ecology of value, Nietzsche's ecology is a positive ecology of value designed to sustain species whose will to power is value-positing:

society must *not* exist for society's sake but only as the foundation and scaffolding on which a choice type of being is able to raise itself to its higher task and to a higher state of *being*—comparable to those sun-seeking vines of Java . . . that so long and so often enclasp an oak tree with their tendrils until eventually, high above it but supported by it, they can unfold their crowns in the open light and display their happiness.[71]

It is Nietzsche's commitment to an ecology of value that makes him an antisocial thinker. The boundaries of society must be constricted in order to sustain the flower of value. For the anti-Nietzschean, however, the argument will go the other way. The boundaries of society must be extended in order to decrease the possibility of value.

A Possibility

Nietzsche's image of the vine climbing the oak neatly encapsulated his idea that the Supermen must exercise their will to power as parasites upon society. Translating the idea into historical terms supplied Nietzsche with an extraordinary vision: 'I see in my mind's eye a *possibility* of a quite unearthly fascination and splendour . . . a spectacle at once so meaningful and so strangely paradoxical it would have given all the gods of Olympus an opportunity for an immortal roar of laughter—*Cesare Borgia as Pope*.'[72] Like the vine that strangles the tree as it reaches toward the sunlight, Cesare Borgia would have abolished Christianity by becoming its head.

The totalisation of society does not require such fantasies, but it may involve changes for which many are unprepared. For example, one recent appeal for the ongoing totalisation of society is 'The Declaration on Great Apes', which proclaims that

The notion of 'us' as opposed to 'the other', which like a more and more abstract silhouette, assumed in the course of centuries the contours of the boundaries of the tribe, of the nation, of the race, of the human species, and which for a time the species barrier had congealed and stiffened, has again become something alive, ready for further change.

The Declaration looks forward to 'the moment when the dispersed members of the chimpanzee, gorilla and orang-utan species can be liberated and lead their different lives as equals in their own special territories in our countries'.[73] However, neither the signatories of the Declaration, nor subsequent advocates of simian sovereignty, have specified where these simian homelands should be located. It has been suggested that some heavily indebted equatorial nation might be induced to cede part of its territory in return for relief from its creditors.[74] But within a negative ecology of value there may be other, more appropriate solutions.

Even if not undertaken with this intention, extending the boundaries of society to include members of other species is liable to devalue specifically human values, notably those of culture. Not only does it run counter to the Nietzschean argument that (super) humans, as the sole value-creating species, should live in a world that maximises their capacity to flourish at the expense of other, non-value-generating species, but by including within society so many unregenerate philistines, it undermines the capacity for human culture to function as a shared value within the expanded society. In such a philistine ecology, some redundant piece of the West's cultural heritage might prove to be a suitable location for an autonomous simian group. Perhaps the Louvre and its collections could be put at the disposal of apes freed from zoos and research laboratories: the long galleries could be used for sleeping and recreation, the Jardin des Tuileries for foraging.[75] Who but a Nietzschean could object?

3

Negative Ecologies

The desert is growing. How far can it spread?

Ernst Jünger

Nietzsche's treatment of nihilism is often surprising, not least in its transformation of a relatively recent neologism into a world-historical category. The portrayal of Bazarov in Turgenev's *Fathers and Sons*, published in 1862, had given the concept currency.[1] But it was the assassination of Tsar Alexander II in 1881 (which also led to the death or execution of all the plotters) that gave the question of nihilism an immediate political urgency, and it was in the years following this event, to which he alludes as 'nihilism à la St Petersburg—(meaning the *belief in unbelief* even to the point of martyrdom)', that Nietzsche turned his attention to the theme.[2]

He was not alone. In the 1880s, nihilism was the subject of several books in Germany, and the topic of excitable commentary throughout Europe and the United States. Nietzsche's interest should therefore be seen in the context of a wave of international anxiety akin, perhaps, to the fascination with Islamic terrorism since 2001. This, too, had racial undertones: the *New York Times* described the Russian nihilists as 'Asiatic Nomads seeking to destroy Western Civilization', and there was frequent reference to their 'Tartar' origins.[3] Describing Bakunin, one French writer offered the view that 'this man was certainly not a European, a Slav, a child of the Aryan deists, but a descendant of the atheist hordes who have nearly destroyed our world several times already, and who, instead of the idea of progress, carry the idea of nothingness buried in their hearts'.[4]

Above all, the sudden eruption of this new threat to the established order required explanation, and this was also Nietzsche's question: 'Nihilism stands at the door: whence comes this uncanniest of all guests?'[5] But his answer is novel. Unlike his contemporaries, he finds the origins of nihilism not on some remote steppe but within European civilisation, and not among the conquering hordes, but in what he calls 'the slave morality'. For Nietzsche it is 'the inexorable progress of the morality of compassion . . . the most uncanny symptom of the uncanny development of our European culture' that has led towards nihilism.[6] The explanation for its appearance lies in the Christian-moral interpretation of the world.[7]

'*Nihilist und Christ*: they rhyme, and do not merely rhyme,' Nietzsche claims.[8] But why should Christianity result in nihilism? What Nietzsche calls 'the first nihilism' is simple pre-ideological despair induced by the hardships and uncertainties of existence. Christian morality was 'the great *antidote*' to such nihilism in that it prevented man from despairing of himself by affirming the existence of another world, and a set of values, at odds with those of this world.[9] Yet by positing a true world in opposition to this one, Christianity was itself an attempt to negate the world by overcoming it.[10] In this way, Christian morality also potentially legitimated the critique of its own, otherworldly values in the name of truthfulness. Such a critique was inevitable, because the values of Christian morality are self-denying, and the only consistent alternatives are either to renounce those values or to renounce the self. Hence the appearance of what Nietzsche termed 'the terrifying Either/Or' that might confront coming generations: 'Either abolish your reverences or—*yourselves*! The latter would be nihilism; but would not the former also be—nihilism?—This is *our* question mark.'[11]

Varieties of Nihilism

Much of Nietzsche's later writing is an attempt to resolve this dilemma: how to find a route out of nihilism not itself nihilistic. Finding such a route is difficult for two reasons: on the one hand, because nihilism is not yet completed, attempts to end it may serve only to effect its continuation; on the other, because it has more than one form, attempts to evade one may fall into the embrace of the other.

Nietzsche claims that there are degrees of nihilism; that it is increasing, and that the increase is inevitable. Although we live, at present, in the midst of what he calls 'incomplete' nihilism, 'complete nihilism is the necessary consequence of the ideals entertained hitherto'.[12] Nihilism works through history because it has an inexorable internal logic. It represents 'the ultimate logical conclusion of our great values and ideals'.[13] The history of the next two centuries can be related in advance for 'necessity itself is at work here'. Attempts to escape nihilism without revaluing our values so far 'produce the opposite, make the problem more acute'.[14] This process will inevitably continue until we reach the most extreme nihilism, one that places the value of things not in any corresponding reality, but 'in their being merely a symptom of strength on the part of the value-positers'.[15] Only then, when it has moved beyond value to valuation, is nihilism complete, and only then will it be possible to move beyond it.

If it is impossible to go beyond nihilism until it is complete, how does Nietzsche think it is to be completed? Although he does not always differentiate between them, Nietzsche suggests that throughout nihilism's history there are two tracks. On the one hand, there is 'Nihilism as a sign of increased power of the spirit: as *active nihilism*'; on the other, 'Nihilism as a decline and recession of the power of the spirit: *passive nihilism*'. Active nihilism 'can be a sign of strength: the spirit may have grown so strong that previous goals ("convictions", articles of faith) have become inadequate'.

Passive nihilism, on the other hand, may be seen as 'a sign of weakness. The strength of the spirit may be worn out, exhausted, so that previous goals and values have become inappropriate and are no longer believed'.[16] In the former case, strength has increased to the extent that 'it no longer requires these total interpretations, and introductions of meaning', whereas in the latter there is no longer enough 'creative strength to create meaning'.[17]

The distinction between active and passive nihilism also has a historical dimension, in that both forms are susceptible to differences of degree. There are thus potentially four ideal types of nihilism: incomplete passive; incomplete active; complete passive; and complete active. Although Nietzsche does not set them out systematically, and his vocabulary contains considerable ambiguity, all four types can be identified within his writings: incomplete passive nihilism is represented by Christianity; incomplete active nihilism is referred to as 'active nihilism' and is associated with overt destruction of an anarchist type; a more complete passive nihilism is found in Buddhism; while a completed active nihilism, sometimes referred to as 'extreme nihilism', is embodied by the Superman, Nietzsche's metaphor for the 'higher type' of the future.[18] The four ideal types potentially generate six points of comparison, and we can use this rubric to contextualise Nietzsche's repeated contrasts between them.[19]

The primary distinction between passive and active nihilism, as it exists in the present, is between Christianity as an incomplete form of passive nihilism that still retains an adherence to values, in this case the values of the weak, and the incomplete active nihilism that has developed from it, as a result of the rejection of those values. According to Nietzsche, Jesus was the type of man who, if he appeared in Europe today, 'would live, teach, and speak as a nihilist', and 'Christianity . . . is in the profoundest sense nihilistic' in that it denies this world and the natural values of the strong.[20] For those who have come off badly, Christian morality is a form of protection against despair at their own oppression. But this morality only induces despair in the strong, who end up denying Christian values themselves. This is active nihilism, and the context in which this appears is the opposite of that which gave rise to passive nihilism. Whereas Christianity is a remedy applied at profound levels of misery, active nihilism appears under conditions that are much more favourable.[21]

This explains the appearance of active nihilism in contemporary Europe, where the extreme position represented by Christianity has been replaced not by 'moderate ones but by extreme positions of the opposite kind':[22] for example, the nihilism that is standing at the gate, created by a backlash from 'God is truth' into the fanatical belief 'All is false'.[23] Both the Christian and the anarchist are 'set only on destruction', but of the two it is the stronger spirit of the latter that demands 'the No of the deed'.[24]

As Nietzsche makes clear, Christianity is not the only nihilistic religion. All religion is, by definition, nihilistic, but the other faith with which he compares Christianity is Buddhism. Christianity and Buddhism have some important things in common. Both are forms of passive nihilism in that they implicitly or explicitly agree that it is 'better *not* to be than to be',[25] and both are said to have 'owed their origin and above all their sudden spread to a tremendous collapse and disease of the will'.[26]

From *The Birth of Tragedy* onwards, Buddhism is associated with the 'negation of the will', and, following Max Müller's essay on Buddhist nihilism of 1869, Nietzsche identifies this negation with nihilism.[27] However, whereas Christianity had tried and failed to produce an antidote to nihilism through establishing an alternative system of values, Buddhism has moved beyond values altogether: 'Buddhism . . . no longer speaks of "the struggle against *sin*" but, quite in accordance with actuality, "the struggle against *suffering*" . . . it stands, in my language, *beyond* good and evil.'[28]

Christianity represents the perspective of an 'unproductive, suffering kind, a kind weary of life' who think that 'this world, in which we live, is an error—this world of ours ought not to exist', but nevertheless maintain that 'the world as it ought to be exists'. In contrast, Buddhism represents 'the same species of man, grown one stage poorer, [who] no longer possessing the strength to interpret, to create fictions' has become a thoroughgoing nihilist, that is, 'a man who judges of the world as it is that it ought *not* to be, and of the world as it ought to be that it does not exist'.[29]

Buddhism therefore represents a move toward the completion of passive nihilism. Whereas Christianity established civilisation as a means of taming the strong, 'Buddhism is a religion for the end and fatigue of a civilisation'.[30] Its reemergence in Europe portends a 'nihilistic catastrophe that puts an end to earthly culture'.[31]

Buddhism differs from Christianity in its refusal of substitute values in favour of a negation of valuation itself. But if, on the one hand, Buddhism is an emancipation from value, it is also a renunciation of the active destruction of value. It therefore differs from active nihilism both in that active nihilism is concerned with the negation of values, and in that it 'achieves its maximum of relative force as a violent force of destruction'. The opposite of such active nihilism is a 'weary nihilism that no longer attacks: its most famous form Buddhism; a passive nihilism'.[32]

The distinction between active nihilism and Buddhism can become confused because in some places Nietzsche uses Buddhism simply as a synonym for nihilism, as, for example, when he complains that the howling 'anarchist dogs' and democratic socialists alike threaten Europe with 'a new Buddhism'.[33] Similarly, he imagines a European Buddhism that takes the form of active nihilism. The nihilism that believes everything is false is associated with a 'Buddhism of the *deed*'.[34] To what does this refer? Not to a passive nihilism, like classical Buddhism, that implies 'one must not act',[35] but rather to an active nihilism of a particular kind. '*Buddhismus der That*' is an unmistakable reference both to the anarchist tactic of 'Propaganda of the deed', '*Propaganda der That*', and to the suicidal '*Nihilismus der That*' that Christian values prevent, but which active nihilism's rejection of those values would permit.[36]

So, while classical Buddhism leads directly to annihilation through the will to nothingness, active nihilism does so indirectly through deliberate provocation. These are the nihilists who 'destroy in order to be destroyed', who want to compel 'the powerful to become their hangmen'. This is 'the European form of Buddhism, *doing No* after all existence has lost its "meaning"', represented by those St Petersburg nihilists, who Nietzsche said had taken 'belief in unbelief even to the point of martyrdom'.[37]

Nietzsche differentiates between forms of nihilism in terms of the diverging responses to 'the world as it is', on the one hand, and 'the world as it ought to be' on the other. Christianity answers No to the first and Yes to the second. Active nihilism and Buddhism respond negatively to both. But the Superman says Yes to the world as it is and No to the world as it ought to be—a move that effectively overcomes the distinction between the two, by implying that the world is already as it ought to be.

This is the significance of eternal return, 'existence as it is, without meaning or aim, yet recurring inevitably', a doctrine Nietzsche repeatedly refers to as 'the most extreme form of nihilism'.[38] It presupposes the denial of 'the world as it ought to be' made by Buddhists and active nihilists alike, but at the same time opens the way for a more positive response to the world as it is:

> whoever has really . . . looked into, down into the most world-denying of all possible ways of thinking—beyond good and evil and no longer, like the Buddha and Schopenhauer, under the spell and delusion of morality—may just thereby, without really meaning to do so, have opened his eyes to the opposite ideal: the ideal of the most high-spirited, alive, and world-affirming human being who has not only come to terms and learned to get along with whatever was and is, but who wants to have *what was and is* repeated into all eternity.[39]

Buddhism had moved beyond value to valuation, but, faced with the terrible possibility of eternal recurrence, had chosen annihilation, the denial of valuation itself. In contrast, the Superman embraces valuation in the full awareness that there are no values, and no possibility that the world will ever be other than it is.

The doctrine of eternal recurrence also serves to distinguish the active nihilist from the Superman. In the context of eternal recurrence, 'coming off badly' takes on a new significance. No longer simply a matter of political domination, it also refers to those who are psychologically, or, as Nietzsche has it, 'physiologically', unable to cope with the idea: 'they will experience belief in the eternal recurrence as a curse, struck by which one no longer shrinks from any action'.[40]

Active nihilism may, as Nietzsche claims, be a sign of strength relative to the weakness of passive nihilism, but it is, simultaneously, 'a sign of the lack of strength to posit for oneself, productively, a goal, a why, a faith'. It 'represents a pathological *intermediate state* . . . because the creative forces are not yet strong enough'.[41] If they were stronger, they would be able to move beyond values, for 'it is a measure of the degree of strength of will to what extent one can do without meaning in things'.[42]

The Superman therefore differs from the active nihilist in the same way that the Buddhist differs from the Christian: the Christian and the active nihilist are still concerned with values, while the Buddhist and the Superman have moved beyond values to valuation. However, whereas the Buddhist moves beyond the Christian because he no longer possesses the strength for valuation, the Superman moves beyond values because he has greater strength, which allows him to posit values in the face of eternal valuelessness.

Because the Superman combines maximum strength and maximum negativity, he is doubly differentiated from Christianity, which is characterised by a system of values generated by weakness. It is the Superman's strength that allows him to do without values, accept that 'valuation itself is only this will to power', and nevertheless go on valuing. Indeed, where value is 'merely a symptom of strength on the part of the value-positers', it could not be otherwise.[43]

It is for this reason that Nietzsche answers the question 'Who will prove to be the *strongest?*' with the surprising but, to his liberal admirers, reassuring reply, 'the most moderate, those who do not require any extreme articles of faith'.[44] However, this is not a new philosophy of moderation,[45] but, as its context within the Lenzer Heide fragment makes clear, the acceptance of the most extreme hypothesis of all.

The history of nihilism is, for Nietzsche, the history of extremity. To the first nihilism of routine suffering, Christianity had offered an alternative, 'God'. This was 'far too extreme a hypothesis', but it was replaced by one that was equally extreme, the 'in vain' of present-day (i.e. active) nihilism. Taken to its logical conclusion this 'in vain' is expressed in the doctrine of eternal recurrence, 'the most extreme form of nihilism'.[46]

Faced with meaninglessness eternally, the strongest are those who can accept it without any correspondingly extreme reaction. Their moderation consists in their ability to live with eternal recurrence without direct or mediated self-destruction, without succumbing either to the Buddhist will to nothingness, or to the active nihilists' compulsion to bring about their own execution. It is in this, and this alone, that the moderation of the strongest is to be found.

The most moderate are therefore to be found not between extremes, but at the furthest extreme, for they alone can live with the most extreme hypothesis (eternal recurrence). Hence Nietzsche can elsewhere describe the same position in terms of its extremity:

We immoralists—we are today the only power which needs no allies in order to conquer: thus we are by far the strongest of the strong . . . A powerful seduction fights on our behalf . . . The spell

that fights on our behalf, the eye of Venus that charms and blinds
even our opponents, is the *magic of the extreme*, the seduction that
every extreme exercises: we immoralists, we are . . . extreme.[47]

After Nihilism

Where does Nietzsche locate himself within this history? In several
places at once: both before and after nihilism, sometimes anticipat-
ing its arrival, as European culture moves 'in what direction?
Towards a new Buddhism? Towards a European Buddhism?
Towards—*nihilism?*'; sometimes awaiting its end, and the 'man of
the future, who will redeem us . . . from the will to nothingness,
from nihilism'; sometimes looking back over its completed history,
describing himself as having 'lived through the whole of nihilism,
to the end, leaving it behind, outside himself'.[48]

He writes in a sort of now-time where all options are simultaneously available: 'a soothsayer-bird spirit who *looks back* when
relating what will come'. He does not place himself within a linear
process, so much as in a complex relation to a multiplicity of points,
contrasting his revaluation of all values with its predecessor, active
nihilism, its putative rival, the passive nihilism of Buddhism, and,
above all, with its double opposite, the passive nihilism of
Christianity, with which it has neither activity nor the (dis)value
of valuation in common.

The progression from incomplete to completed nihilism and
beyond is also temporal. The first phase, that of incomplete nihilism, is the phase of values: the negative values of Christian
morality, and the negation of those values by active nihilists. The
former have been dominant for almost two millennia, but, as
events in Russia suggest, the latter is already emerging as a coun-
terstrategy. The second phase, in which nihilism is completed, is
concerned with valuation rather than values. Although something
like the Buddhist negation of the will has already been espoused by

Schopenhauer, Nietzsche clearly thinks of this as an as yet unrealised, terminal phase of European civilisation. But this too could be
a transitional stage:

> Every major growth is accompanied by a tremendous crumbling
> and passing away: suffering, the symptoms of decline *belong* in the
> times of tremendous advances; every fruitful and powerful
> movement of humanity has also created at the same time a nihilistic
> movement. It could be the sign of a crucial and most essential
> growth, of the transition to new conditions of existence, that the
> most extreme form of pessimism, genuine *nihilism,* would come
> into the world.[49]

Nietzsche plans to move beyond it while presupposing it: 'Such an
experimental philosophy as I live anticipates experimentally even
the possibilities of the most fundamental nihilism; but this does not
mean that it must halt at a negation, a No, a will to negation. It
wants rather to cross over to the opposite of this—to a Dionysian
affirmation of the world as it is.'[50] Those who can face eternal
recurrence without either the Buddhist's longing for annihilation
on the one hand, or the active nihilist's destructive self-destruction
on the other, will finally have left nihilism behind.

Valuation

What does nihilism mean? That 'the highest values devaluate
themselves'.[51] The history of nihilism's completion is therefore the
story of the progressive devaluation of value. But how does that
history relate to the history of value itself? Does the renunciation
of value make the world any more or less valuable? Although the
set of opinions about the amount of value in the world may be
quite independent of the actual value of the world, in Nietzsche's
account they cannot be separated. Accepting the consequences of
nihilism means accepting that the world has no value except that

imputed to it, and that value is merely a 'symptom of strength on the part of value-positers'. The history of value therefore dissolves into the history of valuation, and valuation into life, for valuation is only will to power, and will to power is 'life itself'. [52]

However, it does not automatically follow that the spread or completion of nihilism diminishes the value of the world. Nietzsche is adamant that '*the total value of the world cannot be evaluated*'.[53] He offers two justifications for this claim. First, that 'there is no totality' and no evaluation can be made 'in regard to something that does not exist'.[54] On this view, the world as a whole has no summative value, because the herd, 'the *sum of zeroes*', counts for nothing in itself, and 'the value of the units determines the significance of the sum'.[55] Second, that even if one could speak of a totality, its total value would necessarily be constant or unknowable; given that 'becoming is of equivalent value every moment: the sum of its values remains the same, in other words it has no value at all'.[56]

Although there may be no totality because mankind is not a whole, there is, nevertheless, a system in which the ascent of one unit is related to the descent of others: 'an inextricable multiplicity of ascending and descending life-processes'.[57] There is no total value, but there is what Nietzsche terms a 'general economy of the whole'.[58] How does this work? It is, in the most literal sense, a set of zero-sum relationships, for 'one furthers one's ego always at the expense of others'.[59] A higher type is possible 'only through the subjugation of the lower',[60] and when a lower type ascends, as happened with the abolition of slavery, it is at the expense of the strong.[61] In effect, therefore, the extent of any advance can be 'measured according to the scale of the sacrifice required'.[62] And it is on this account that 'in the general economy of the whole the terrible aspects of reality are to an incalculable degree more necessary'.[63]

For Nietzsche, there are no values as such, and the totality of value is the totality of valuation. There is no way to evaluate the total value of the world itself, but there are ways of measuring fluctuations in the totality of valuation in the world. Valuation is life itself, and within this totality the units that count are those in ascent. Since ascent is relative to that over which there is ascendancy, the value of any unit is derived from the cost to others. Unlike the exploiters, the exploited and the unexploited are zeroes who count for nothing in themselves. If the numbers of those exploited remain the same, then the total value of the whole will remain constant. But where there is less than maximal exploitation then the value in, but not strictly of, the totality is less than it could be.

Ecologies of Value

Nietzsche's account of nihilism is therefore synchronic as well as diachronic. Putting the diachronic and the synchronic together, the transition from incomplete to a complete nihilism represents a movement within the economy of value. It is an economy realised through the ecology of living beings, so the history of nihilism is the history of populations living together across time. Changes in the extent and nature of nihilism come about through the disappearance, destruction, or development of different types of nihilist, and it is through that ecology that the history of nihilism is played out.

Nietzsche makes several explicit references to the way in which this ecology works. The first offers an explanation of the causes of nihilism:

> The higher species is lacking, i.e., those whose inexhaustible fertility and power keep up the faith in man [e.g. Napoleon].
>
> The lower species ('herd', 'mass', 'society') unlearns modesty, and blows up its needs into cosmic and metaphysical values. In this way the whole of existence is vulgarised: in so far as the mass is dominant, it bullies the exceptions, so they lose their faith in themselves and become nihilists.[64]

In this case, Nietzsche describes a situation in which the demographic imbalance between the higher and the lower species results in the spread of nihilism among the former. Elsewhere, he goes on to describe a point at which nihilism is reached, and 'all one has left are the values that pass judgement—nothing else'. This has differing effects on those with differing degrees of strength:

> The weak perish of it.
> Those who are stronger destroy what does not perish.
> Those who are strongest overcome the values that pass judgement.[65]

So although nihilism is caused by the preponderance of lower types, it results in their destruction. This is especially true of the most extreme nihilism, embodied in the doctrine of eternal recurrence:

> The unhealthiest kind of man in Europe (in all classes) furnishes the soil for this nihilism; they will experience the belief in the eternal recurrence to be a curse, struck by which one no longer shrinks from any action; not to be extinguished passively, but to extinguish everything that is so aim- and meaning-less, although this is a mere convulsion, a blind rage at the insight that everything has been for eternities—including this moment of nihilism and lust for destruction.—It is the value of such a crisis that it purifies, that it pushes together related elements to perish of each other . . . it also brings to light the weaker and less secure among them, and thus promotes an order of rank according to strength, from the point of view of health: those who command are recognised as those who command, those who obey as those who obey.[66]

The weak are the passive nihilists, extinguished passively; those who are stronger and destroy what does not spontaneously perish are the active nihilists who no longer shrink from any action but destroy in order to be destroyed. Those who command are those whose acceptance of eternal recurrence allows them to survive the crisis, the Supermen.

The crisis is not exclusively intellectual. Being active means 'reaching out for power', being passive means 'to be hindered from moving forward'.[67] The two movements are related: reaching out for power involves hindering others; being hindered means being hindered by others. The one necessarily implies the other: 'What do *active* and *passive* mean? Do not they signify becoming *master* and being *defeated*?'[68] These are, however, trajectories, not identities. Becoming master and being defeated are relational. The strong are strong insofar as they gain ascendancy over the weak; the weak are weak in that they are defeated.

After 'the period of catastrophe' and the 'advent of a doctrine that sifts men',[69] there will, Nietzsche hopes, be a third ecology— one where differential breeding maintains a more stable balance between higher and lower types. Here too, Nietzsche thinks in terms of the totality: 'To what end shall "man" as a whole—and no longer as a people, a race—be raised and trained?'[70] His consistent answer is that 'perfecting consists in the production of the most powerful individuals, who will use the great mass of people as their tools'.[71] So the only uncertainty is how to 'sacrifice the development of mankind to help a higher species than man come into existence'.[72]

His suggestion is to take advantage of the 'dwarfing and adaptation of man to a specialized utility' effected by capitalist modernity, and use this as a base on which to create a higher form of mankind:

> This higher form of aristocracy is that of the future. —Morally speaking, this . . . represents a maximum in the exploitation of man: but it presupposes a kind of men on whose account this exploitation has meaning. Otherwise, it would really be nothing but an overall diminution, a value diminution of the type man—a regressive phenomenon in the grand style.[73]

Here, then, is Nietzsche's third ecology. The first, which generated (passive) nihilism, was produced by an excess of lower types;
the second, the crisis of nihilism, prompted by the emergence of
some stronger types (active nihilists), serves to get rid of that
excess through a mix of voluntary and involuntary annihilation;
the third embodies the productive equilibrium represented by
maximal exploitation.

Ecologies of Valuation

Each of these is an example of an ecology of value in the sense that
it generates certain positions within the history of values that is
nihilism, but it is also an ecology of value in that an ecology is, for
Nietzsche, what value ultimately is—not a set of values, or even of
valuations, but rather a set of circumstances:

> The standpoint of 'value' is the standpoint of conditions of
> preservation and enhancement for complex forms of relative life-
> duration within . . . becoming.

> 'Dominating forms'; the sphere of that which dominates continually
> growing or periodically increasing or decreasing according to the
> favourability or unfavourability of circumstances.

> 'Value' is essentially the standpoint for the increase or decrease of
> these dominating centres.[74]

What are these dominating forms, *Herrschaftsgebilde*? Nietzsche
specifically distinguishes the 'theory of dominating forms' from
mere 'sociology', which was, he said elsewhere, 'the sum of zeroes'.[75]
The theory of dominating forms is the theory of the forms created
by the trajectories that count, trajectories of ascent. Yet the forms to
which he refers are not individual trajectories themselves, but rather
the shapes collectively created by them. Such forms are not unities

but multiplicities made up of infinitely divisible points of will 'constantly increasing or losing their power'.[76]

However, such dominating forms do take on definable shapes. Though Nietzsche sometimes used the word *Herrschaftsgebilde* to refer to the priestly power structures of the Christian church,[77] his primary point of reference is the new aristocracy of the future. There are, he suggests, two futures for humanity, one 'the outcome of mediocratisation', the other 'conscious distinction, self-shaping'. The latter preserves the highest and lowest species, but destroys the middle one.[78] The theory of 'dominating forms' is therefore a theory of aristocracy; the perspective of value is that of the waxing and waning of the uppermost species relative to the lowest; and a positive ecology of value is one that provides the conditions for the preservation and enhancement of a new aristocracy.

As the *Genealogy of Morals* makes clear, it has usually been 'some horde or other of blond predatory animals, a race of conquerors and masters' that becomes 'a *living* form of domination', spontaneously shaping both themselves and the shapeless mass of the population. A work of art without an artist, such dominating forms are also 'the most involuntary, most unconscious artists';[79] it is they who work 'as artists on "man" himself'.[80] Value increases when there are 'more favourable preconditions for more comprehensive forms of domination'.[81] And it is to this possibility that Nietzsche refers when he writes that 'the world might be far more valuable than we used to believe'. The source of added value is the doctrine of eternal return: 'that which set apart the higher men from the lower, the desires that create clefts'.[82] Nihilism, the devaluation of existing values that culminates in the doctrine of eternal return, therefore ultimately has the paradoxical effect of bringing about a revaluation in which the value of the world is recognised to be the positive ecology of value brought about by nihilism itself.

It is this ecology that permits Nietzsche to emerge from nihilism. Yet moving beyond completed nihilism is a double manoeuvre: it is not in value-positing that value ultimately resides, but (and this is the bit his defenders do not like) in the particular ecology that allows it. Why? One overcomes nihilism by disregarding value and placing a positive valuation upon valuation. Valuing is will to power, which means power over, and hence there can be no value where there is no power over. In consequence, there is more value in an unequal society than an equal one. Those who value valuation are the new aristocracy, but the value of their valuation of valuation lies not in that valuation itself but in the social arrangement it effects, which is the only one that permits valuation to take place at all.

Although Nietzsche locates this ecology beyond the history of nihilism, further developments within that history might reopen the story. Nietzsche's great insight is that nihilism is the product of failure as much as scepticism. On the one hand it is part of the history of a scepticism propelled by the logic of negation; on the other it is part of a negative ecology, the unintended consequence of failure. To the question: how far can the desert spread, there are potentially two answers: until there is nothing left to negate, and until the conditions are maximally unconducive to value-positing.

These are not mutually exclusive possibilities, for one produces the other. It is an important part of Nietzsche's critique of existing values that he reveals that their latent function is to have a negative effect on the ecology of value, and he implicitly (or explicitly) makes this his central argument against them. At the same time, he suggests that they are the consequence of a particular ecology. Nietzsche offers more than one account of this process, a process that provides a model for what could be a fourth ecology, a negative ecology, not of value but of valuation.

A negative ecology is produced by the logic of negation represented since the French Revolution by anarchists, peaceful revolutionaries, and socialists who 'are at one . . . in their thoroughgoing and instinctive hostility to every other form of society except that of the *autonomous* herd (even to the point of repudiating the very concepts of master and servant)'.[83] However, it is also the consequence of the formation of such a society, in that such revolutionary doctrines embody just the degree of scepticism necessary to justify and protect the herd of human failures. Socialism is 'the logical conclusion of the *tyranny* of the least and the dumbest'; in which 'is hidden, rather badly, a will to negate life'.[84] The two go together: 'to us the democratic movement is not only a form of decay of political organization but . . . the diminution of man, making him mediocre and lowering his value'.[85]

For Nietzsche, the present ecology is characterised by its mixed character: there is continuing exploitation, but the morality of compassion has led to the enervation of the strong and the proliferation of lower types. From this position he envisages two alternative futures: a great crisis that leads to a new positive ecology of optimal exploitation, or else a further reduction in exploitation and the resulting spread of mediocrity. In the former case, extermination is necessary because 'the great majority of men have no right to existence, but are a misfortune to higher men'.[86] A surplus of unexploited lower types is a negative weight on the total ecology, not only because it will reduce the total amount of exploitation, but also because it may diminish the proportion of exploitation within the society in question and thus change its composition and moral character. Moving towards a positive ecology means reducing that surplus. In the latter case, the proliferation of lower types reduces the proportion of units that count, leaving only what Nietzsche calls 'the tremendous surplus of failures: a field of ruins'.[87]

Beyond the Last Man

Nietzsche considers the latter a real possibility.[88] But how? Although Nietzsche does not appear to have considered its consequences at the time, he describes it happening in the prologue to *Zarathustra*. Having delivered his prophetic vision of the Superman, Zarathustra warns the crowd that although there is still time for the vision to be fulfilled, it will not always be so: 'the soil is still rich enough for it. But . . . [it] will one day be poor and weak; no longer will a high tree be able to grow from it'. That poor soil is the Last Man—among whom there is no herdsman and one herd because 'everyone is the same'. He has barely finished his account when 'the shouting and mirth of the crowd interrupted him. "Give us this Last Man, O Zarathustra"—so they cried—"make us into this Last Man, O Zarathustra! You can have the Superman!"'[89]

The move made by the crowd is an example of 'reading like a loser'—interpreting the possibilities offered by the text to one's own disadvantage. This is not a matter of espousing or denying specific values, or having a positive or negative valuation of anything, including the value of valuation or even the value of devaluation; it is merely a matter of assuming a trajectory. In this case, presented with the alternatives of paths that lead toward the Superman and the Last Man, the latter 'a laughing stock, or a painful embarrassment', the crowd turns away from the Superman towards the Last Man.

What does that turn represent? The Superman and the Last Man do not constitute concurrent alternatives within Nietzsche's ecology of value, in that they represent mutually incompatible possibilities. (An ecology that sustained the Superman could not accommodate the Last Man, and vice versa.) Rather, they represent a choice between trajectories. This choice is similar to, but not the same as, that represented by Nietzsche's challenge 'Either abolish your reverences or—*yourselves*', which presented to the Christian the alternatives of either an active nihilism or a more consistent passive nihilism of the kind represented by Buddhism. However, reading like a loser is not a counter-ethic like that of Christianity, nor a will to destruction like that of the Buddhist. Neither value-positing nor annihilationist, it is a failure beyond death, a staying alive in order to grow weaker.

In making this choice, the reader also makes a move within Nietzsche's economy. The object of the choice does not define the move; it is the trajectory embodied by making one choice rather than the other, the orientation of the self within the individual movements of ascent and descent that make up the economy of value. For Nietzsche, to read like a loser is to become one. Zarathustra tells the crowd: 'The Superman is the meaning of the earth. Let your will say: The Superman *shall* be the meaning of the earth!' By opting for a descending trajectory independently of the ascending trajectory of the Superman, the crowd opts for preemptive defeat, a failure that creates losers without victors: surplus failures.

However, the herd, the sum of zeroes, is not necessarily the most negative ecology possible. An ecology which ensures that everyone is a zero prevents the emergence of both the exceptionally strong and the exceptionally weak: 'The instinct of the herd considers the middle and the mean as the highest and most valuable . . . [and] feels the exception whether it be below or above it, as something opposed and harmful to it.'[90] The herd therefore seeks to defend itself on both sides: against those above, and against 'those who have degenerated from it (criminals, etc.)'. [91]

As Nietzsche here implies, reading like a loser does not necessarily reach its limit with the herd. The social constituency of the herd is variously defined in terms of species (the cow, the lamb, the 'little good-natured sheep'), in terms of social position (the 'people', the 'slaves', the 'plebeians'), or in terms of health ('those who are from the outset victims, downtrodden, broken—they are the ones, the *weakest* are the ones who most undermine life').[92] In every case these are relative positions—relative to predator animals, the aristocracy, or the healthy—though in some cases these are purely relative (predator/prey and master/slave) and in others comparative (healthy/sick).

Egalitarianism ends direct exploitation by bringing the minority of exploiters down to the level of the exploited; it puts an end to purely relative inequality but not to comparative inequality. Even without exploitation there is still a difference between the healthy and the sick, or, as Nietzsche puts it in *Genealogy*, between 'the bell with a full tone' and 'the one which is cracked and out of tune'. Like William Cowper's 'stricken deer, that left the herd', the loser may assume a trajectory of failure relative to the herd itself. This is not necessarily through direct exploitation by the herd: a failure to keep up, an inability to maintain parity with one's equals, is enough for a gap to open up. Within an unequal society, reading like a loser increases equality. Within an equal society, reading like a loser is always undermining egalitarianism, threatening to defeat equality through simple failure. As such, it is the route not only to equality, but also beyond it, to the extraegalitarian, to the less than zero.

Nietzsche notes that 'There is a point in the history of society when it becomes so pathologically soft and tender that among other things it sides even with those who harm it, criminals, and does this quite seriously and honestly.'[93] Reading like a loser takes society to just this point (and beyond), continually devaluing the herd by slowing it to a pace slower than that of the weakest member acknowledged to remain within it. If egalitarianism produces (and is produced by) a society that no longer has the strength to exploit, extraegalitarianism produces a society in which no one is left behind, or, as Nietzsche puts it, 'a society that no longer has the strength to *excrete*'.[94]

A Lower Species

A society that cannot excrete will poison itself, for it is a society in which there is a negative ecology of value, a society that generates nihilism. Could this be what a society is for? And if so, what sort of nihilism is this, and how does it differ from that which Nietzsche thinks he has completed?

For Nietzsche, the negation of value requires valuation, if only in the form of devaluation. In order for there to be (de)valuation there must be valuers and social arrangements that permit (de)valuation to take place. Nihilism, in the form of the individual negation of value, may have no limit in terms of the values that may be negated, but it does have a limit in terms of the ecology that will sustain (de)valuation. Nihilism is individual and its limit is social.

Assuming that nihilism requires nihilists, Nietzsche does not distinguish a society that generates nihilists from a society that generates nihilism. It is this that allows him to uncouple the ecology of nihilism from the ecology of value and argue that an ecology of nihilism is ultimately a positive one because it sustains the most perfect nihilists possible. But Nietzsche also allows us to see beyond this argument. If nihilism is the devaluation of value, where value is merely the ecology that permits devaluation, value is devalued not by a valuer devaluing the value in question, but by a reduction in the overall capacity for valuation or devaluation to take place.

Although produced by individual failure, such nihilism is social rather than individual in form, in that what is specifically nihilistic about it is its negative impact on the ecology of (de)valuation. Paradoxically, therefore, this is an ecology in which scepticism defines rather than extends the scope of nihilism. Individual scepticism reaches its limit in the ecology needed to maintain it; failure, which undermines that ecology, is also potentially limitless. But not all failure is nihilistic; it furthers the history of nihilism only insofar as it undermines whatever is currently of value—in this case, the ecology of extreme scepticism itself. Even so, on this account, the desert can always spread a little further. In the process, it leaves some of nihilism's characteristic features behind, for this is a nihilism that spreads without nihilists, a nihilism that cannot articulate its own scepticism.

Nietzsche's question can now be restated: could one sacrifice the development of mankind to help a lower species than man come into existence? Perhaps. In *Zarathustra*, the Voluntary Beggar says that 'If we do not alter and become as cows, we shall not enter into the kingdom of heaven.'[95] Seeking to learn from them, he had been talking to the cows for half the morning, and they were 'just about to reply' when Zarathustra's arrival interrupted the conversation.

We can discover what they might have said from an earlier passage, in the essay on 'The Uses and Disadvantages of History for Life':

> Consider the cattle, grazing as they pass you by . . . This is a hard sight for man to see, for . . . a life neither bored nor painful, is precisely what he wants, yet he cannot have it for he refuses to be like an animal. A human being may well ask an animal: 'Why do you not speak to me of your happiness but only stand and gaze at me?' The animal would like to answer, and say: 'the reason is I always forget what I was going to say', but then he forgot this answer too, and stayed silent: so that the human being was left wondering.[96]

4

Subhumanism

Il faut s'abêtir.

Pascal

Of Nietzsche's interpreters, the one who does most to engage with and perhaps even to develop his account of nihilism is Heidegger. It is an engagement internal to the intellectual history of fascism in both context and subject. Heidegger's series of lectures on Nietzsche were given between 1936 and 1940 (and, when delivered, though not when published in 1961, contained topical references to the early progress of the war); the two major essays on closely related themes 'The Word of Nietzsche: "God is Dead"' and 'Nihilism as Determined by the History of Being' were begun later in the conflict (in 1943 and 1944 respectively); the 'Letter on Humanism' was composed in the immediate aftermath, when Heidegger was still banned from teaching, while the final essay in this sequence, 'On the Question of Being', was written in 1955 in response to Ernst Jünger—the radical conservative intellectual whose technocratic vision of the Superman had been the original stimulus for Heidegger's interest in Nietzsche.[1] Heidegger later presented this twenty-year confrontation as having distanced him from Nietzsche, and, by implication, as having separated him from his earlier Nazi commitments. But detailed analysis of the texts suggests that, rather than finding his own way, Heidegger ends up following, and indeed taking a little further, a path established by Nietzsche himself.

Although Heidegger eventually argues that Nietzsche does not grasp nihilism when he describes it, but rather embodies it when he tries to overcome it, he does not reject Nietzsche's distinction between incomplete and completed nihilism:

> Incomplete nihilism . . . replace[s] the former values with others, but still posits the others in the old position of authority . . . as the ideal realm of the suprasensory. Completed nihilism, however, in addition must do away even with the place of value itself, with the suprasensory as a realm, and accordingly must posit and revalue values differently.[2]

However, whereas much of Nietzsche's writing about nihilism is concerned with forms of nihilism other than his own, the prehistory of his perfected nihilism as it were, Heidegger is concerned not with that prehistory but almost exclusively with Nietzsche's own form of nihilism. One result of this is that passive nihilism, in the form of Christianity and Buddhism, quickly disappears from the narrative, allowing Heidegger to focus on the development of Nietzsche's 'active-extreme, ecstatic-classical nihilism'.[3] This is said to progress from extreme nihilism, which 'recognizes that there is no "eternal truth in itself"', to active nihilism, which abolishes the realm of the suprasensuous and 'acknowledges truth as a configuration of will to power', to ecstatic nihilism, which 'affirms the *"principle of value-estimation"*, to wit, the will to power', to classical nihilism, 'the "ideal of supreme powerfulness"', which expressly conceives the will to power as the ground of all valuation and 'grants whatever wants to die its "longing for the end"'.[4]

Nevertheless, nihilism as a whole always remains ambiguous. For Heidegger, as much as Nietzsche, it comprehends both the devaluing of the highest values up to now, and the unconditional countermovement to devaluing. The former phase is summed up in the statement 'God is Dead', which, according to Heidegger, is tantamount to saying that 'Western philosophy understood as

Platonism . . . is at an end.'[5] The underlying opposition is therefore between metaphysics, i.e., any philosophy in which the 'whole
is differentiated into a sensory and a suprasensory world and the
former is . . . determined by the latter', and nihilism, which implies
that 'Nothing is spreading out' where "Nothing" means . . . [the]
absence of a suprasensory, obligatory world'. The completion of
nihilism therefore involves both the rejection of metaphysics and
the substitute values of incomplete nihilism. This process is,
Heidegger suggests, 'the fundamental movement of the history of
the West', whose unfolding, he writes ominously in 1943, 'can have
nothing but world catastrophe as its consequence'.[6] For Heidegger
as for Nietzsche, nihilism is a world-historical question.

Inversions

Alongside these gloomy reflections, Heidegger retains the idea
that nihilism calls for freedom from values as a step towards the
revaluation of values,[7] and, like Nietzsche, sees the process of
revaluation as being formed by that of devaluation. His argument
here is considerably more ornate, if not ultimately more complex,
than that of Nietzsche himself.

The nihilist is 'the denier of the distinction between true and
apparent worlds and the hierarchy of values posited in it'. But it
does not follow from this that the apparent world is abolished
alongside the true. The antithesis of the apparent world and the
true world may, as Nietzsche claims, reduce itself to the antithesis
of 'world' and 'nothing', and that might suggest that both are
'dissolved into nothingness', but, according to Heidegger, that is
not the case. He demonstrates the point with reference to truth,
value, power, and Being.

On the one hand, 'truth as error is a *necessary value*' in that it is
unavoidably part of 'the essential constituency and essential activity of life'. On the other, the apparent world, which naturally arises
from the activity of whatever is alive, can no longer be understood

as mere semblance, even though it '*is* only *what* and *how* it arises'.[8]
This formation and transformation of appearances is what we call
art, not art conceived as aesthetic pleasure, but art as what 'secures
life perspectivally in its vitality, that is, in the possibilities of its
enhancement'.[9] Nietzsche claims 'We possess art lest we perish of
the truth',[10] and Heidegger glosses this by arguing that art functions as the complement of truth, so that at the same time as the
true world is reduced to one of appearances, the apparent world
becomes in effect true, with the paradoxical result that the true and
the apparent worlds exchange places. Truth has become error, but
we need error in order to live, and so generating errors, forming
the world of appearances through art, becomes the only truth we
have.[11]

Similarly, it might appear that 'if all barriers between truth and
untruth fall and everything is of equal value', everything is then of
no value.[12] Not so, according to Heidegger. Nietzsche suggests
that though the true world is devalued, rather than everything
becoming of no value, a revaluation takes place in which valuation
becomes a value instead. The argument here parallels that with
regard to truth and appearance. Existing values may be valueless,
but the world itself is still there and 'presses inevitably on toward a
new positing of values'.[13] The devaluation of values therefore leads
to a revaluation of the nature and manner of valuing, with the
paradoxical outcome that 'Nihilism itself is thus transformed into
the "ideal of a superabundant life".'[14]

It is in this light that Heidegger interprets Nietzsche's statement
that value is 'the standpoint of conditions of preservation and
enhancement for complex forms of relative life-duration within . . .
becoming'.[15] Nietzsche himself focuses on the conditions that allow
one life form to dominate at the expense of another, whereas Heidegger
unpacks the significance of the preservation-enhancement conjunction in terms of the relationship between a given quantum and that
which exceeds it: 'Preservation and enhancement mark the fundamental tendencies of life, tendencies that belong intrinsically

together.' Of the two, he suggests, it is the latter that is the more fundamental.[16] This, he argues, is what is involved in the will to power: 'Power is power only if and as long as it is enhancement of power . . . To the essence of power pertains the overpowering of itself.'[17]

As this makes clear, Heidegger interprets the relationship of truth to art, and value to value-positing, in the same way, equating the first term in each pair with preservation, the second with enhancement.[18] On this basis, he argues that art can be identified with will to power: art 'is the essence of all willing' and it 'excites the will to power first of all toward itself and goads it on to willing out beyond itself'.[19] Similarly, 'Will to power and value positing are *the same*, insofar as the will to power looks toward the viewpoints of preservation and enhancement.'[20]

Art, value-positing and will to power are therefore effectively interchangeable in that within each pair of terms—truth and art, value and value-positing, power and will—nihilism undermines the former, but cannot do so without invoking the latter, so revealing the latter to be the essence both of itself and of the former term. Will to power is not then a matter of striving to come into power: 'What the will wills it does not merely strive after as something it does not yet have. What the will wills it has already. For the will wills its will. Its will is what it has willed. The will wills itself.'[21]

If nihilism leaves us with art, valuation, will, where does it end? At its most extreme, nihilism comes down to a choice between not willing and willing nothing. Of the two, 'The will shrinks, not from nothingness, but from *not willing,* from the annihilation of its ownmost possibility', for 'the will to nothingness still permits willing—that the will itself be'.[22] To will nothingness is to will that nothing will be different, in other words, the eternal return of the same.[23] To will it for all things is not to will it for one form of life, but for the flux of becoming itself. So the supreme will to power, willing nothingness, 'comes to pass when transiency is represented as perpetual Becoming in the eternal recurrence of the same, in this way being made stable and permanent'.[24] This, to quote a line from Nietzsche cited repeatedly by Heidegger, is 'To stamp Becoming with the character of Being'.[25]

Heidegger construes this as another play of preservation-enhancement. Here, however, the starting point is different. Rather than reducing preservation to enhancement, the eternal return starts from the premise that all is enhancement and tries to preserve that process of change:

> The sense is not that one must brush aside and replace Becoming as the impermanent . . . with Being as the permanent. The sense is that one must shape Becoming as Being in such a way that as *becoming* it is preserved, has subsistence, in a word, *is*. Such stamping, that is, the recoining of Becoming as Being, is the supreme will to power.[26]

History of Nothing

According to Heidegger, Nietzsche imagines that 'thinking *Becoming* as the *Being* of the totality of beings, thinking "will to power" in terms of the "eternal recurrence of the same"', is a form of nihilism so extreme 'that it is no longer even a nihilism'.[27] But it is precisely this that allows Heidegger to turn the tables on Nietzsche's self-appointed role as the thinker in whom nihilism is consummated and overcome.

How does the argument work? Heidegger specifies that nihilism proper is a function of nothing. It means 'Nothing is befalling everything and in every respect', in other words, that 'Nothing is befalling Being itself.'[28] In which case, although nihilism might indeed exist where nothing is happening to beings, its essence appears only 'when the *nihil* concerns Being itself'. The essence of nihilism is 'the history in which there is nothing to Being itself'.[29]

That history can be traced in the history of Western philosophy, where 'what is, is thought in reference to Being; and yet the truth of Being remains unthought'.[30] In Nietzsche, this pattern is repeated. Like his predecessors, he not only does not think the truth of Being, but also disguises the fact. In Nietzsche's case this happens through the devaluation and revaluation of values, in which thinking 'whatever is, in its Being, as the will to power . . . necessarily thinks it as value positing'.[31] Yet at the same time, Nietzsche elevates value-thinking to a principle. So, Being remains unthought because the Being of beings is reduced to becoming, while the acceptance of the eternal return stamps Becoming with the character of Being, so disguising the denial of the thinking of Being involved in the former move.

Nietzsche believes he overcomes nihilism 'in the positing of new values from the will to power', which proclaims that 'there is nothing to Being itself which has now become a value'. In fact, this shows 'not only that Nietzsche's nihilism does not overcome nihilism but that it can never overcome it'.[32] In making Being a value, Nietzsche fails to 'recognize the Being of beings, and indeed It itself, *Being*, specifically as *Being*'.[33] This non-recognition is itself an example of nothing befalling Being itself, and as such places Nietzsche's thought squarely within the tradition he aspires to move beyond: that Nietzsche interprets Being as a value 'is the effectual, actual omission of the default of Being itself in its unconcealment'.[34] Nietzsche's nihilism is therefore merely 'the *fulfilment* of nihilism', an example of what it purports to overcome.[35]

However—and this is the paradox that gives Heidegger's argument a twist worthy of a thriller—the nature of Nietzsche's failure to overcome nihilism shows the fundamental opposition between nihilism and metaphysics to have been illusory. Metaphysics may posit the suprasensory and nihilism its absence, but in approaching Being from the standpoint of beings, metaphysics makes Being into a being in its turn.[36] To 'stamp Becoming with the character of Being' is what metaphysics has always done, thinking 'what is . . . in reference to Being'. For this reason 'Being itself necessarily remains unthought in metaphysics', which means, of course, that *'metaphysics as such is nihilism proper'*.[37] Nietzsche's completion of nihilism therefore takes him no further than the beginning of metaphysics. He 'thinks Being in a thoroughly Platonic and metaphysical way', for 'the metaphysics of Plato is no less nihilistic than that of Nietzsche'.[38]

The essence of nihilism is not its opposition to metaphysics, but the fact that in nihilism *'Nothing* is happening to Being'.[39] This implies that the histories of nihilism and Being cannot be separated, that 'nihilism would be in its essence a history that runs its course along with Being itself', and perhaps more surprisingly that the history of nihilism is the history of Being, because the nothing that happens to Being happens in nihilism itself. In metaphysical thought, which is co-extensive with nihilism, nothing is taken to mean that 'there is nothing to the being as such', without any awareness 'that Being itself stays away *in the very priority of the question about the being as such'*.[40]

In which case, the role of nihilism within the history of Being is as paradoxical as that of Being within the history of nihilism. For just as the essence of nihilism is not nothing, but rather nothing as the default of Being, so the essence of Being is not something, but rather its default, a withdrawal played out within the history of nihilism. Indeed, for Heidegger, it lies 'in Being's own essence . . . that Being remains unthought because it withdraws'.[41] The essence of nihilism and the essence of Being are therefore effectively one: *'The essence of nihilism proper is Being itself in default of its uncon-cealment, which is as its own "It", and which determines its "is" in staying away.'*[42]

Ecology of Being

Where does this surprising conclusion leave the history of nihilism as a historical phenomenon? Will it ever end? According to Heidegger, nihilism is authentic when it 'is the default of Being itself'. However, 'such authenticity is not admitted *as* the authenticity of nihilism'. Nihilism fails to acknowledge its own failure to notice the default of Being. In this way, Heidegger argues, it 'omits even the omission of its own act'. So, ironically, 'the authenticity of nihilism is *not* something authentic', in that 'it takes the form of inauthenticity which accomplishes the omission of the default by omitting this very omission'. This is metaphysics. Metaphysics is 'the inauthenticity in the essence of nihilism', and 'the full essence of nihilism is the original unity of its authenticity and inauthenticity'.[43]

Understood in these terms, any attempt to overcome nihilism would mean that man of himself advances against Being in its default, because nihilism, if it is authentic, is Being in its default. This venture would be both quixotic and, ultimately, self-defeating, for it would involve remaining heedless of the history of Being unfolding within that of nihilism (that 'Being itself has brought it to pass that there is nothing to Being itself'). In other words, it would omit the omission and so lapse into metaphysics, just as Nietzsche does. According to Heidegger, 'all wanting-to-overcome puts nihilism behind us, but only in such a way that . . . nihilism rises up around us unperceived, ever more terrible in its power'.[44]

Instead of trying to overcome nihilism/metaphysics, Heidegger suggests that it is necessary only 'to encounter Being in its default as such', to become aware that even in the omission of the omission Being 'promises itself in its unconcealment'.[45] This means thinking to encounter 'the advent of the self-withdrawal of Being in relation to its abode; that is to say, the advent of the essence of historical man'. Such an encounter requires an awareness that, even as staying away, Being 'lays claim to the essence of man. That [that] essence is the abode which Being itself provides for itself, so that it might proceed to such an abode as the advent of unconcealment.'[46]

And what is the essence of man? In the 'Letter on Humanism', Heidegger challenges the Aristotelian idea of man as *animal rationale*. Man is not only a living creature who possesses language along with other capacities. To think of man this way is to 'abandon man to the essential realm of *animalitas* even if we do not equate him with beasts but attribute a specific difference to him'. This is what happens in metaphysics which 'thinks of man on the basis of *animalitas* and does not think in the direction of his *humanitas*'.[47] In contrast, Heidegger suggests that the essence of man 'lies in his ek-sistence' where the ek-sistence of man is 'standing in the clearing of Being'. Language creates this possibility, for 'language is the house of Being in which man ek-sists by dwelling, in that he belongs to the truth of Being, guarding it'.[48]

However, Heidegger is at pains to emphasise that 'Man is not the lord of beings. Man is the shepherd of Being . . . [with] the essential poverty of the shepherd, whose dignity consists in being called by Being itself into the preservation of Being's truth'.[49] That poverty is a function of Being's withdrawal, a poverty which, like the humble stove to which Heraclitus invited his visitors with the words 'Here too the gods are present', does not preclude the presence of Being but rather conveys its promise. This conclusion has obvious implications with regard to the limits of nihilism:

> Thinking does not overcome metaphysics by climbing still higher, surmounting it, transcending it . . . thinking overcomes metaphysics by climbing back down . . . the descent leads to the poverty of the ek-sistence of *homo humanus*. In ek-sistence the region of *homo animalis*, of metaphysics, is abandoned . . . To think the truth of Being at the same time means to think the humanity of *homo humanus*.[50]

Heidegger draws out the implications of this in 'On the Question of Being'. Jünger, quoting Nietzsche's remark about having lived through the whole of nihilism and put it behind him, had challenged Heidegger to consider what might be beyond nihilism, 'over the line', 'across the meridian'. Heidegger responded with an essay, also originally titled *Über die Linie*, but with the sense of *de linea* rather than *trans lineam*. There can, he argues, be no crossing over, just a going over, at the most, a crisscrossing. Jünger, in his eagerness to leave nihilism behind, carries it with him into the future, just as Nietzsche had done. But there can be no overcoming when nihilism has not even been apprehended for what it is—the nothing that happens to Being, and therefore part of the history of Being itself. And that awareness 'can be attained only when . . . the essence of the nothing in its former kinship with "Being" can arrive and be accommodated among us mortals'.[51]

The so-called line is not, as Jünger has it, something external to the human essence which we, as individuals or as a civilisation, can cross when the moment comes; it is rather the human essence itself: 'The human being not only stands *within* the critical zone. He himself . . . is this zone and thus the line.' It is in this space that nothing happens to Being, an event Heidegger here represents for the first time typographically by the crossing out of the word Being, to show that the human being belongs to the nothing, 'to the essence of nihilism and thereby to the phase of its consummation'.[52] On this understanding, it is in the human essence that '~~Being~~ remains absent' and 'conceals itself'. Yet at the same time, this 'concealing of the as yet unrevealed essence . . . of ~~Being~~, shelters untapped treasures and is the promise of a find that awaits only the appropriate seeking'. The human being 'holds the place of the nothing', which is why, of course, it also holds the place of Being.[53]

Negative Ecology of Being

Does Heidegger's response to nihilism differ from Nietzsche's? In both cases, the human forms the limit. Heidegger presents the human essence as the centre around which the question of Being turns, but it is also the limit beyond which he refuses to go, for by making the human essence into the line, Heidegger effectively posits it as that beyond which nihilism cannot pass without turning back on itself—given that nihilism, as the default of Being, is already constitutive of that essence.

Although Heidegger might appear to be rejecting humanism, it is opposed only 'because it does not set the *humanitas* of man high enough'.[54] The human essence alone stands in relation to Being. To 'represent the human being as one particular entity among others (such as plant and animal)' is too inclusive.[55] Standing 'in the clearing of Being' is a 'way of being . . . proper only to man'. The clearing, as the open, 'shelters and salvages Being', and 'man and he alone sees into the open'.[56] Other living creatures are separated from it by 'an abyss'. Lacking language, they inhabit their respective environments but are 'never placed freely in the clearing of Being which alone is "world"'.[57]

When Heidegger makes statements such as 'Language is the house of Being. In its home man dwells', or ' "world" is the clearing of Being into which man stands out on the basis of his thrown essence',[58] these are specifically statements about human beings as opposed to other living creatures. Language is uniquely human, and world is something to which other entities do not have the same kind of access. As he had earlier argued in *The Fundamental Concepts of Metaphysics*, compared with the human being 'The animal is poor in world, it somehow possesses less . . . of what is accessible to it.' Unlike a stone, it has access to beings, but does not have access to beings *as* beings, which is 'something that *only we* are capable of', but is rather 'captivated' by them.[59] Whereas the human has world (is 'world-forming'), the animal is world-poor, and the stone worldless.

This suggests that in taking his distance from Nietzsche, Heidegger may be continuing his trajectory. Both Heidegger and Nietzsche rely on transcendental arguments based on whatever is assumed in negation. Nietzsche's analysis of nihilism comes to rest when, using value as a pivot, it reaches an ecology of value-positing produced through an inverse relation between the devaluation effected through the completion of nihilism in the eternal return, and the positive ecology of valuation that effects it. Heidegger suggests through a far more complex pattern of mediations an inverse relation between devaluation effected through nihilism and the self-revelation (through concealment) of Being. For Heidegger the negation of Being requires an ecology of openness to Being. And because 'the question of the nothing puts us, the questioners, in question', '*one* being always keeps coming to the fore in this questioning: the human beings who pose this question'.[60] That is, human beings as opposed to other living creatures.

Avoiding any immediate reaffirmation of the positive, both Nietzsche and Heidegger argue that nihilism leaves only the ecology required to sustain nihilism itself. Nietzsche moves from the negation of value to a positive ecology of valuation, Heidegger from nothing spreading out to a positive ecology of Being. Both posit that nihilism requires something to be found within specifically human existence, and therefore an ecology that can be sustained only by the flourishing of a particular species. The line on which the history of nihilism starts to turn back on itself is the line of species difference. And insofar as that line is the limit of nihilism, the very possibility of a limit hinges upon it.

Nietzsche argues that the ability to accept the eternal return depends upon a positive ecology of valuation to sustain the Supermen who alone accept it. Since value-positing is a ratio between super- and sub-human, such an ecology is susceptible to the continuation of nihilism through the creation of a surplus of subhumans. In contrast, Heidegger thinks of ecology in terms of ontology and the relationship between Being and beings. Like Nietzsche's, Heidegger's argument assumes a positive ecology— not of valuation but of Being. What would a negative ecology of Being involve in this case? It might be supposed that it involved moving the line, or at least a change in the ratio of those on either side. But there is not a direct analogy with Nietzsche here, for Heidegger's ecology does not depend on maintaining a particular ratio between the human and the nonhuman, and it would be affected by changes in the relative numbers of the two groups only if humans threatened to disappear altogether.

Heidegger's negative ecology would take a different form. His definition of nihilism—nothing is happening to Being—is presented as nihilism's ultimate negation. In fact, it is used to set a limit on nihilism by making it axiomatic that nothing does not happen to anything other than Being. According to Heidegger, Being and nothing 'are not given alongside one another'; rather there is a giving of both Being and nothing together.[61] Not only is nothing the way that Being happens, it is the only way that nothing happens, and so there is no negation without promise. In a negative ecology, however, nothing would be given without Being, and there would be negation without promise. Is this possible? ~~Being~~ implies a constant and equal self-undermining, but even if you cannot have erasure without the word, the relation between the two might change: Being might fade away or the crossing out grow more emphatic. The separation of Being and nothing, or the waxing of one and the waning of the other, is what potentially creates such an ecological change, and if nothing extends its reach while Being remains constant, the change is a negative one.

By arguing that nihilism is nothing spreading out, and that nothing is something that happens to Being, Heidegger deduces that nihilism is something that happens to Being and so can extend no further than Being itself. Yet he also quotes approvingly Leonardo's dictum 'The nothing has no middle, and its limits are the nothing.'[62] This implies that nothing is borderless. In which case, where nihilism is nothing spreading out, might it not seep beyond the line? There are two ways to think about this. If Being and nothing are not coextensive and coequal then there could be nothing without Being, and if they are coextensive and coequal there might nevertheless be some possible experience that was not the nothing without Being, but rather of something less than nothing. Might Heidegger's account be open to either or both of these possibilities?

Darkening

For Heidegger, as for Nietzsche and Jünger, the history of nihilism unfolds in the intellectual and political history of the West. Following Nietzsche, Heidegger uses a variety of words to refer to this 'darkening'.[63] Its essential features are 'the flight of the gods, the destruction of the earth, the reduction of human beings to a mass, the preeminence of the mediocre'.[64] Heidegger equates this 'darkening of the world' (*Weltverdüsterung*) with the abandonment of Being. Not only is 'the abandonment of Being brought nearer by being mindful of the darkening of the world', but the 'specific elucidation of the abandonment of Being is the derangement of the West; the flight of the gods . . .', etc.[65] Darkening is clearly another way of describing the process through which 'nothing is spreading out'.

How far can the darkening spread? Darkening is of its very nature a difference of degree, a diminishing ratio of light to dark. As such, it always presupposes the simultaneous presence of light. 'Darkness (*Dunkelheit*) is a manner of "being away" . . . [its] being consists in being potential daylight . . . The dark also lets things be seen.'[66] On this interpretation, darkening is confined to the clearing of Being. Rather than being obscured by it, the clearing's presence is indicated by the darkness: 'A clearing in the forest is still there even when it is dark . . . Darkening (*Verdunkeln*) does not encroach upon the clearing. The clearing is the presupposition for getting light and dark.'[67] But does this mean that wherever there is darkness there must be a clearing? Is it not dark in the forest too?

Heidegger is ambivalent on this point. The clearing of Being is world, and so the darkening must at least be able to spread as far as the world. And what is world? 'When we speak of the darkening of the world . . . [it] is always *spiritual* world. The animal has no world (*Welt*), nor any environment (*Umwelt*).'[68] On this account, the darkness can spread only as far as the animal, for the animal has no world to darken. And yet in his account of the world-poverty of the animal, Heidegger suggests that there is a sense in which 'the animal has world'. Indeed, world-poverty is constituted by the having and not-having of world. This then raises the question of how world-darkening and world poverty connect. Would the world darken as world-poverty spreads?

On the basis of the passage cited above, Derrida claims that world-darkening has nothing to do with the world-poverty of animals.[69] But Heidegger elsewhere clouds the issue. In *Contributions to Philosophy* he discusses 'Darkening and worldlessness', noting that 'the rock is not even worldless, because it is indeed without darkening'. This clearly implies that if (as he elsewhere asserts) the rock were indeed 'worldless', let alone 'world-poor', it would be darkened. Heidegger uses a different word for darkening here, *Erdunkelung*, a neologism derived from *Verdunkelung*. But this is not, as the formation of the word might imply, a darkening of the earth as opposed to the world, for it is specifically identified as being (like *Weltverdüsterung*) impossible without world. At the same time, it is equated with the animal's experience of world-poverty, for 'the first darkening' is 'grounded in the captivation of what is alive'. Here darkening and the captivation that is characteristic of animal behaviour go together, linking the darkening to instinct and the priority of the species. Rather than presupposing the clearing, darkening here goes along with 'falling-back from the incipient opening'.[70]

If the animal has world might it not also be susceptible to the darkening, and if it does not, how are we are to describe its experience of lack? Either animals experience some form of darkening, or they have some other experience that is of an exclusion from darkness. Translated into terms of Being and nothing, there are three possibilities: (i) animals have an experience of nothing that is, like that of the human being, an experience of the abandonment of Being; (ii) they have an experience of nothing that is not of the absence of Being; (iii) they have some experience which is less than nothing, a sort of outer darkness. In the first case, Heidegger's distinction between humans and animals would break down; in the second, the animal would undermine Heidegger's claims regarding the coequality and coextension of Being and nothing; in the third, the animal's experience would justify the claim that nihilism might continue beyond nothing into an outer darkness.

Ratio/Line

The source of this uncertainty lies in Heidegger's account of world-poverty, in which he implies both that there is only a difference of degree between humans and animals, and that there is a difference in kind which makes the 'poverty of the ek-sistence of *homo humanus*' completely distinct from the poverty of the animal.

Heidegger starts from the premise that 'Poor in world implies poverty as opposed to richness; poverty implies less as opposed to more. The animal is poor in world, it somehow possesses less. But less of what? Less in respect of what is accessible to it.'[71] This suggests that poverty is a quantifiable property that might be expressed in terms of a ratio between access and possession, and that the varying ratios in which it occurs might form a continuum on which, at different points, humans and animals might be located. Heidegger himself initially appears to accept the implication:

> If we now look more closely at the distinction between poverty in world and world-formation in this form, this distinction reveals itself as one of degree in terms of levels of completeness with respect to the accessibility of beings in each case. And this immediately supplies us with a concept of world: world initially signifies the sum total of beings accessible to man or animals alike, variable as it is in range and depth of penetrability. Thus

'poor in world' is inferior with respect to the greater value of 'world-forming'.[72]

This would imply that there is one thing, world, of which humans have more and animals less, and this reading is confirmed by Heidegger's later references to the darkening involved in the specific way in which animals apprehend the world.

And yet Heidegger also insists that animals have no world, not in the sense that they do not possess as much world as humans, but rather in that they do not have world at all. On this reading, world refers to 'the manifestness of beings as such as a whole' and is always characterised by this 'wholeness'. In this sense, 'world belongs to world-formation' (because unless formed 'as a whole' there is no world) and world-formation belongs to human beings, for 'Man as man is world-forming'. This does not mean that human beings are human and contingently world-forming, but that world-forming is part of the human essence, without which man would not be man.[73]

Can these two positions be reconciled? Derrida, who repeatedly highlights the tension, claims that Heidegger simply rejects the first hypothesis:

> This poverty is not an indigence, a meagreness of world. It has, without doubt, the sense of privation, of a lack: the animal does not have enough world to be sure. But this lack is not to be evaluated as a quantitative relation to the entities of the world.[74]

However, Heidegger leaves open the possibility of understanding 'the animal's not having of world as a deprivation after all'.[75] And it is clear from later references to darkening that, however much he sought to qualify it, he never entirely disregards the first hypothesis, but rather maintains it alongside the second one.

One way to hold on to both possibilities might be to think in terms of two worlds, W^1 and W^2. In W^1 there is a having *and* not-having of world, a continuum between world-formation and world-poverty in which the latter is just a lesser capacity for the former. In W^2, there is either a having *or* a not-having of world. These are not, however, two distinct worlds, for a particular ratio on the continuum in W^1 acts as the threshold for the change of a state in W^2. This threshold is the line of the human and, as such, also the limit where nihilism turns back on itself. However, this line in W^2 is just a particular but potentially variable ratio in W^1. Darkness cannot spread beyond the line in W^2, but in W^1, the darkness must spread beyond the ratio at the line for the ratio to be meaningful. The problem for Heidegger is that on this interpretation nihilism stops at the line in W^2 but continues beyond it in W^1.

Let us translate the problem into theological terms for a moment. Everyone is to some degree both saint and sinner, but on the judgement day, everyone will be deemed either saint or sinner depending on the degree to which they are saintly and sinful. This has two implications that have troubled theologians: how is it that the sinful can be numbered among the saints, and how is it that the saintly can be numbered among the sinners? Heidegger dwells at length on his equivalent of the former possibility (nihilism in the history of Being) but is ambivalent about the latter. If the threshold for experiencing poverty were lower than that for experiencing promise, there would be a continuum in suffering but not in redemption. Then, as Heidegger acknowledges, 'a kind of pain and suffering would have to permeate the whole animal realm and the realm of life in general', just as in Saint Paul's image of nature yearning for redemption.[76]

Heidegger dismisses this possibility on the grounds that the animal simply does not have world, though on his own account world appears to be given to animals in just this way. World is the clearing of Being; the animal has access to world, but not to the clearing, because it does not possess enough of that to which it has access. That to which it has access, but does not possess, it experiences as captivation—potentially a form of suffering or darkening.

Is this the nothing? The question does not have to be resolved. In W^1 it is the nothing and in W^2 it is the less than nothing; in W^1 it is the darkness, in W^2 the outer darkness. For the purposes of the argument about nihilism, the question of exactly how world-poverty is experienced by the animal is irrelevant. What is important is that nihilism does not have to turn on the line of the human essence, for there is some possible experience beyond the line, an experience more nihilistic than that of the human being at the line.

Might this happen to anyone other than an animal? World-poverty is specifically the space of loss, the space of having and not-having, the space of being called and unchosen. It is reading like a loser that opens up this space. This is what reading like a loser is, by definition. Reading like a loser is just a failure to form the world.

Transposedness

Heidegger himself explores this possibility without fully realising its implications in his discussion of transposedness, his term for the possibility of experiencing the world as someone or something else experiences it. However, he emphasises that this does not mean 'the factical substitution of oneself for another so as to take its place', nor, on the other hand, a merely hypothetical ' "as if" . . . in which we merely act as if we were the other being'. It involves 'neither an actual transference nor a mere thought-experiment that supposes such transference has been achieved', but a 'going along with what it is and how it is . . . by being ourselves'. [77]

In light of this definition, Heidegger poses a threefold question: Can we transpose ourselves into a stone, an animal, and a human being? In the first case, the answer is clear. It is impossible, for the stone has 'no sphere intrinsically belonging to it' into which we could, even in principle, transpose ourselves. In the third case, the question can apparently be answered in the affirmative, because being able to go along with others is a fundamental feature of human experience. In fact, it is so fundamental that the question cannot even be asked, because being transposed into other human beings 'already and originally belongs to man's essence'.[78]

It is only in the case of animals that the situation is ambiguous. We do not question that, unlike the stone, the animal 'does relate to other beings' and has a sphere of its own, and that 'something like a going-along-with, *a going along with in its access to and in its dealings with its world*' might be possible.[79] Indeed, we comport ourselves toward animals as though we were aware of being already so transposed (just as we do with humans). On the other hand, Heidegger suggests that there is something subtly different about the experience, even with domestic animals, which are closest to us:

> We do not live with them if living means: *being* in an animal kind of way. Yet we *are with* them nonetheless. But this being-with is not an *existing-with* because a dog does not exist but merely lives . . . Does it comport itself toward the table as table, toward the stairs as stairs? All the same it does go up the stairs with us . . . A going along with . . . a transposedness, and yet not.

Heidegger struggles to define what it is 'that grants the possibility of transposedness and necessarily refuses any going along with . . . What is this having and yet not having?' His answer is that it is a form of world-poverty grounded in the essence of the animal: 'the animal has and yet does not have world. This now reveals itself as a potentiality for granting . . . connected in turn with the necessary refusal of any going along with.'[80] This implies that having world is a form of inviting transposedness, while not having world is a form of refusing going along with. The animal both invites and refuses because it has and does not have world. This is logically necessary, because insofar as the animal, like the stone, does not have world, there is literally nothing to go along with. Transposedness and going along with are not two distinct experiences; to be transposed is to go along with. To invite transposition and refuse going along with is not then to invite one thing and refuse another, but to invite and refuse the same thing, the 'and yet not'.

The structure of invitation and refusal therefore reflects that of poverty itself, but in transposedness the human experience of the world-poverty of the animal would be of that same poverty experienced from the outside rather than within, the mirror image of world-poverty, as it were. How might we think of this? In terms of W^1 and W^2, man necessarily cannot experience anything below the line in W^2, for that line is the human essence; in terms of W^1, however, where world is defined by the ratio of possession to access, the human might be able to share that part of the world that the animal does possess rather than merely has access to. Invitation to transposedness would therefore be an invitation to experience the world as a ratio, but at a lower level than the ratio of the line.

However, even if the animal's experience were an experience of the less than nothing rather than the nothing, being transposed into the animal could for a man only be an experience of the nothing. Both because man cannot not have world, and because, insofar as the animal does not have world it must refuse going along with, transposedness is only possible with respect to the animal's having rather than not-having of world. Nevertheless, having world as the animal does is still not an experience of the absence of Being, so if man were to be transposed he would encounter nothing without Being, not in the animal's not-having world but rather in the animal's having it. Invitation to transposedness is an invitation to slip over the line, to experience nothing without Being. Going for a walk with the dog is an ontological risk. Reading like a loser is what the animal invites us to do, and vice versa.

Politics of Failure

Do such metaphysical speculations have any conceivable application? They are the history of the twentieth century. Heidegger's Nietzsche lectures, and the sequence of essays that followed, supposedly distanced the philosopher both from Nietzsche and his earlier entanglement with National Socialism. But this appears to be, at best, only partly true. For in their response to nihilism both Nietzsche and Heidegger rely on what is perhaps the central tenet of fascism in all its forms: the idea that particular human ecologies are the ultimate source of meaning.

In Heidegger's account of Nietzsche's nihilism, the negation of truth finds its end in the fictions of art, the negation of value in value-positing, and the negation of Being in perpetual becoming. Heidegger's response is to argue that Nietzsche's claim that nihilism is transcended in art, value-positing, and becoming is illusory, for it is just the substitution of becoming for Being, and to claim that this is the overcoming of nihilism is merely to extend its history.

According to Heidegger, the history of nihilism is the nothing spreading out, and as nothing is the absence of Being, it cannot spread further than that from which Being might be absent, i.e., the clearing of Being. World, as the clearing of Being, is what human beings *qua* human beings form, and so nihilism reaches its limit in the human essence. But if that is true, Heidegger's argument against Nietzsche ends in the same place—in the claim that there is something that human beings cannot help doing, whether value-positing or world-forming, which they must do in order for nihilism to spread, and which nihilism can therefore never exceed.

For both Nietzsche and Heidegger, nihilism comes to an end in the ecology of the human. A corollary of this is that another ecology, a subhuman ecology, might sustain nihilism rather than preclude its further spread. This would happen in different ways, however. In Nietzsche's case, because value-positing is will to power and power is power over, a positive ecology depends upon the relation of exploiters to exploited; in Heidegger's, on the relation of Being and nothing. In both, however, a negative ecology is one in which there is an excess, an excess of unexploited lower types, or an excess of nothing over Being. This potential excess is represented by the subhuman: the poor in spirit and the world-poor.

How might such a negative ecology develop? In the *Introduction to Metaphysics* Heidegger himself offers two examples, the first taken directly from Nietzsche:

> Let us consider the earth within the dark immensity of space in the universe. We can compare it to a tiny grain of sand . . . on the surface of this tiny grain of sand lives a stupefied swarm of supposedly clever animals, crawling all over each other, who for a brief moment have invented knowledge.

Seen like this, there are no grounds 'for emphasizing precisely *this* being that is called the human being' any more than any other. But if 'beings as a whole are ever brought into our question . . . this questioning necessarily recoils back from what is asked and what is interrogated, back upon itself'. Then it is the human being that stands out rather than 'some elephant in some jungle in India' or a 'chemical oxidation process on the planet Mars'.[81] It is 'the irruption by one being called "man" into the whole of beings'.[82]

By asking the question of Being, man stands (as Heidegger later puts it) 'in the clearing of Being' (in which case, given that the clearing presupposes darkness, the dark immensity of space beyond it might be better described as an outer darkness). The question of Being is, however, also 'the spiritual fate of the West'. And in a now notorious passage, Heidegger links the 'darkening of the world' to the geopolitical plight of the German people in 1935. The spiritual decline of the West is already advanced, and Germany finds itself caught in the pincers between Russia and America:

> Our people, as standing at the centre, suffers the most intense
> pressure—our people, the people richest in neighbours and hence
> the most endangered people . . . must transpose itself . . . into the
> originary realm of the powers of Being . . . if the great decision
> regarding Europe is not to go down the path of annihilation.[83]

Transposing the German people into the realm of Being by 'asking
the question of Being' is therefore the fundamental condition 'for
subduing the danger of the darkening of the world, and thus for
taking over the historical mission of our people, the people of the
centre of the West'.[84]

Important here is not the immediate political context but the
structure of the argument, and the parallel between the fate of
Germany at the centre of the darkening world and that of human
beings lost within 'the dark immensity of space'. Whatever the
precise nature of the programme Heidegger envisages, it is
designed to secure the openness of Being, to arrest the darkening
of the world, to prevent the nothing spreading out. As such, it 'is
intimately linked to the question of who the human being is', and
serves to arrest the darkening of the world if it is answered '*solely*
on the basis of the question about *Being*' rather than in the way
zoology represents animals.[85] In other words, the German people
may save themselves from the fate of other nations in just the same
way that humans escape the fate of other beings.

What would be the alternative? The question unasked would
not permit the Germans to distinguish themselves from the other
nations, or humans from animals. Then the (outer) darkness would
not stop at the national border, or at the boundary of the species.
The point here is not that Heidegger seems to think of non-
Germans as he does animals; it is rather that he thinks of animals in
the same way as non-Germans. The fate of the Germans is illustra-
tive of that of humans as a whole. If they fail to be human, the
nothing spreads out. The unasked question allows world-darkening and world-poverty to spread, and given that human beings

cannot but ask the question, failure to ask is a failure to be human. The alternative to the German people taking up their historical mission would be a politics of failure, politics as a species-changing practice.

To Rilke's claim that the animal sees the open, Heidegger responds: 'never would it be possible for a stone, no more than for an airplane, to elevate itself toward the sun . . . and move like a lark. But not even the lark sees the open.'[86]

Must we all then become stones? Not yet, not yet . . .

5

Excommunication

Each musician plays his instrument as if he were alone in the world.

Michel Serres

In Hugo von Hofmannsthal's *Letter of Lord Chandos*, the young aristocrat relates a strange sequence of events to his correspondent, Francis Bacon. Already the author of pastoral verse and a Latin treatise, he was entertaining other literary projects when he sank to such an 'extremity of faintheartedness and exhaustion' that he found himself unable to write. Now, he is unable to think or speak coherently about anything at all.[1]

First he lost the capacity to discuss abstract questions, finding an inexplicable uneasiness in uttering words like 'spirit', 'soul', or 'body'. Then he struggled with ethical matters, unable to scold a child without the words disintegrating in his mouth. The affliction 'gradually broadened, spreading like rust', until he could barely participate in normal conversation: 'Everything came to pieces, the pieces broke into more pieces, and nothing could be encompassed by one idea.'[2]

Chandos now leads what he fears is a life of incomprehensible inanity. Although managing to keep up appearances, he finds no significance in human interaction, only in the revelation offered by seemingly insignificant objects and creatures—'a watering can, a harrow left in a field, a dog in the sun, a shabby churchyard, a cripple, a small farmhouse'—whose existence can 'suddenly take on a sublime and moving aura'.[3]

The most vivid and startling of these revelations is of rats dying in a cellar. Having ordered poison to be spread at one of his farms, he is overtaken by a vision of 'the cool and musty cellar, full of the sharp, sweetish smell of poison, and the shrilling of the death cries echoing against mildewed walls'. A mother rat is there, like Niobe surrounded by her children, 'not looking at those in their death agonies . . . but off into space, or through space into the infinite . . . gnashing her teeth as she looked!'[4] This is not an experience of pity, but of something 'much more and much less than pity'.[5]

According to Deleuze and Guattari, Chandos's vision is a para-digmatic example of what is involved in 'becoming animal':

> When Hofmannsthal contemplates the death throes of a rat, it is in him that the animal 'bares his teeth at monstrous fate' . . . It is a composition of speeds and affects involving entirely different individuals, a symbiosis; it makes the rat become a thought, a feverish thought in the man, at the same time as the man becomes a rat gnashing its teeth in its death throes. The rat and the man are in no way the same thing, but Being expresses them both in a single meaning in a language that is no longer that of words . . . *Unnatural participation.*[6]

Such 'unnatural participations . . . are the true Nature spanning the kingdoms of nature'. If 'becoming-inhuman' involves any sort of impoverishment, it is balanced by simultaneously 'becoming-animal'. To lose one nature is to gain another, to enter an interkingdom, involving terms 'that are entirely heterogeneous: for example, a human being, an animal, and a bacterium, a virus, a molecule, a microrganism'. A becoming-animal always involves a pack, or assemblage, formed, developed, and transformed by contagion.[7]

Something like this does happen to Chandos. The Roman orator Crassus had become inordinately fond of a pet eel, and was mocked in the Senate for crying over its death; Chandos, in turn, becomes obsessed with this image of Crassus, until it is fixed in his brain 'like a splinter with everything around it a throbbing, boiling, infection'.[8] It is a contagion that spreads across the centuries—the eel, Crassus, Chandos, maybe Hofmannsthal's readers transfixed by the image of Chandos himself.

And yet Chandos's predicament is more often described in terms of deprivation than contagion or transformation. In the first place this takes the form of a change in his perception. Even his own Latin treatise now looks back at him, 'strange and cold'. Seeing its title mentioned in Bacon's last letter to him, Chandos recalls that 'I did not perceive it right away as a familiar image made of words strung together, but was only able to take it one word at a time, as though I had never seen this combination of Latin vocabulary'.[9] It is not only Latin that is foreign to him. He gradually loses the fluency with words needed to participate in general discussion. Opinions customarily offered 'with the sureness of a sleepwalker' become so challenging that he can no longer express them.[10] Like Tantalus in the underworld, he finds that 'worldly ideas' appear to be within reach, yet retreat when he tries to grasp them, 'the boughs of fruit snatched from my outstretched hands, the murmuring water shrinking from my parched lips'.[11] Chandos is, as Hermann Broch describes him, 'isolated in a rich world to which he no longer finds access'.[12]

To this narrative of loss, Heidegger may be a better guide than Deleuze and Guattari, for Chandos's impoverishment is in many respects akin to the world-poverty of the animal, poor in world because it possesses less of what is accessible to it. What is missing is the as-structure of the world. Heidegger imagines a lizard lying on a rock as being perpetually trapped in just this state of deprivation: 'whatever the lizard is lying on is certainly given *in some way* for the lizard, and yet is not known to the lizard *as* a rock'. This is not to imply that it is given to the lizard as something else, rather that 'whatever it is is not accessible to it *as a being*'. The essential characteristic of world-poverty is that 'the possibility of apprehending something as something is withheld'.[13]

It is this difficulty that afflicts Chandos. Both his loss of fluency in the use of words and concepts, and his inability to take his perceptions for granted, are the result of no longer being able to understand something as something. Seeing the title of his treatise, he is unable to apprehend it as the title of *his* treatise, or even as a title, but instead struggles to take it in one word at a time. Heidegger describes how without the 'as', 'we merely stare' with the result that 'our just-having-it-before-us lies before us *as a failure to understand it anymore*'.[14] This is Chandos's fate. He finds himself seeing things as though they were 'terrifyingly close':

> Once I saw through a magnifying glass that an area of skin on my little finger looked like an open field with furrows and hollows. This was how it was for me with people and their affairs. I could no longer grasp them with the simplifying gaze of habit . . . Isolated words swam about me; they turned into eyes that stared at me and into which I had to stare back.[15]

Chandos is deprived of what he once had, and suffers the consequent bewilderment, whereas Heidegger's animals are deprived only of what they might have, and unaware of their disorientation.[16] But the result is similar, a state Heidegger refers to as captivation. Captivation signifies 'having every apprehending of something as something withheld', with the direct consequence that 'in having this withheld from it, the animal is precisely taken by things'.[17] Deprivation and captivation here go together in that captivation occurs just insofar as response to a stimulus is unmediated by meaning. A moth that flies straight into a light 'plunges into the light precisely because it does not attend to the light or grasp it as such'.[18]

In a similar way, Chandos finds himself unexpectedly fixated by particular objects, 'totally at the mercy of . . . their unassailable hostility, their incomprehensibility, their irony'.[19] He describes how as he rides past his tenants standing at their doors, he is actually looking through them, 'searching among all the shabby and crude objects of a rough life for that one whose unprepossessing form . . . can become the source of that mysterious, wordless, infinite rapture'. Even some distant image, like the rats in the cellar, or the story of Crassus, can become the object of an almost obsessional preoccupation, 'a kind of feverish thinking', as though 'an inexpressible something forces me to think about this figure'.[20]

Chandos's captivation should, as Heidegger says of the animal's, not be interpreted simply as 'a kind of rigid fixation', as if spellbound. It is a 'redirecting of the animal's driven activity in accordance with certain instincts' disinhibited by external stimuli. It is what enables the animal to engage in complex forms of behaviour, without the benefit of language, by becoming open 'to that for which it is open'.[21] In Chandos's case, he becomes open to that which he would otherwise see as ludicrous or contemptible, and at the same time experiences 'thinking in a medium more direct, fluid, and passionate than words', a language that is not a language, 'a language of which I know not one word, a language in which mute things speak to me'.[22]

Put in Heidegger's terms, Hofmannsthal's thought experiment is an experience of transposition. Chandos both loses his customary fluency of perception and speech and experiences a revelatory affinity with objects, akin to captivation. He is captivated by animals (and other seemingly trivial objects) not because he is 'becoming-animal', or empathetically identifying with some particular animal, but rather because he is going along with, generically, the animal: a 'going along with what it is and how it is . . . by being ourselves'.[23] In effect, Chandos is transposed into world-poverty as himself, in just that state of deprivation from which humans are, according to Heidegger, ontologically excluded.

Nothing in Common

What is the nature of the worldless world that opens up for Chandos? Of what manner of social life might this poverty be constitutive? For Deleuze and Guattari, becoming-animal involves becoming part of a pack or assemblage. They see Chandos as entering an interkingdom of terms linked by contagion: 'rats are rhizomes' and 'any point of a rhizome can be connected to anything other', like rats swarming over each other.[24] But Chandos's experience is not contagious in the same way. He does not find rats in the watering can, just 'a water beetle sculling on the surface'.[25] Crassus may be captivated by the eel and Chandos by Crassus, but Chandos is not captivated by the eel. The eel does not touch him. His experiences are isolated and intransitive.

From the perspective of Alphonso Lingis, on the other hand, Chandos might appear to have joined a 'shadow community'. In *The Community of Those Who Have Nothing in Common*, Lingis suggests that when we move 'beyond the communication with one another through signals', we may instead 'make contact with inhuman things by embracing their forms and their matter', rather in the way that Chandos, losing his grasp of human language, is intensely engaged by rats and watering cans. Through this process, there forms 'the other community', the double or shadow of the rational community. It forms not in having or producing something in common, but 'in exposing oneself to the one with whom one has nothing in common'. It is 'the community of those who have nothing in common', or, at least, the community 'of those who have nothingness, death, their mortality in common'.[26]

Lingis's account of shadow community is based on Jean-Luc Nancy's distinction between a community founded on common being and a community where there is no common being, merely a being-in-common. The former is a 'communion of singularities in a totality superior to them',[27] whereas the latter is 'existence inasmuch as it is *in* common, but without letting it be absorbed into a common substance'.[28] According to Nancy, recent history attests overwhelmingly to the failure of the former ideal:

> Generations of citizens and militants, of workers and servants of the States have imagined their death reabsorbed or sublated in a community, yet to come, that would attain immanence. But by now we have nothing more than the bitter consciousness of the increasing remoteness of such a community, be it the people, the nation, or the society of producers . . . the communion to come does not grow distant, it is not deferred: it was never to come; it would be incapable of coming about or forming a future. What forms a future, and consequently what truly comes about, is always the singular death.[29]

In other words, the underlying reason that community, in the sense of common being, 'a communion that fuses the *egos* into an *Ego* or a higher *We*', has not taken place is that it is necessarily impossible. Genuine community is inevitably 'the community of mortal beings', which, being made up of finite entities, is necessarily a 'community of *others*.' Hence, paradoxically, 'community is made of what retreats from', with the result that what is lost, 'the immanence and intimacy of a communion', is lost only 'in the sense that such a "loss" is constitutive of "community" itself'.[30]

Nancy's account of the loss that is constitutive of community is the foundation of Lingis's suggestive phenomenology, and a formative text for the work of Agamben and others. Might it provide an adequate account of Chandos's loss, a social ontology of world-poverty? Nancy suggests that as community recedes, 'the common human condition turns up everywhere, more manifest and barren than ever.'[31] Does becoming world-poor, shedding everything that might be shared with others, leave the loser with just that finitude that constitutes being-in-common? And, if so, is this where nihilism ends?

Being-With

It might appear that those with nothing in common must have at least existence in common, and this is Nancy's argument:

> What could be more common than to be, than being? We are. Being, or existence, is what we share. When it comes to sharing non-existence, we are not here. Nonexistence is not for sharing. But being is not a thing we could possess in common. Being is in no way different from existence, which is singular each time. We shall say then that being is not common in the sense of a common property, but that it is in common. Being is in common.[32]

Being in common involves what Nancy terms (with no preferred syntax) being singular plural. '*Being singular plural* means [that] the essence of Being is only as coessence . . . If Being is being-with, then it is, in its being-with, the "with" that constitutes Being; the with is not simply an addition.' For example, 'What I have in common with another Frenchman is the fact of *not* being the same Frenchman as him, and the fact that our "Frenchness" is never, nowhere, in no essence, in no figure brought to completion.'[33] Similarly, what is in common with another being is not being the same being, but the fact that our being is not the *same* being.

For Nancy, community is nothing more than 'the "with" that constitutes it, the *cum* of "community"'. This 'with' has no meaning; it merely signals our co-appearance, our *compearance*, alongside one another. All that is shared is what makes sharing possible—the inescapable fact of finitude. And, as Nancy emphasises, 'finitude itself *is* nothing'; it is just where one thing 'finishes itself . . . where it is-with'. So the with as with is nothing, and the nothing is the 'with', for 'The non-Being of Being, its meaning, is its disposition. The *nihil negativum* is the *quid positivum* as singular plural, where no *quid*, no being, is posed *without with*.'[34]

The nothing that is happening to being is therefore just its disposition, its being singular plural, the 'with'. To those, like Nietzsche, who stand at the final limit of nihilism Nancy therefore offers the confident advice: 'Go all the way, cross over the limit of nihilism, but don't save it. One might say: take a step into nothing (and there is not even a step . . .).' Rather than being a step beyond, the step beyond the limit is a step back, for nothing, the with, is already presupposed in existence itself:

> Meaning finds completion in the extreme form of nihilism: and loses itself in so far as it is meaning. But this loss is no longer nihilistic . . . Instead of meaning, there is strictly no longer nothing and so not even the darkness. That is to say, in reality, there never was nothing . . . There was always existence, the singular plural of existence . . . There is nothing to save: nothing is lost.[35]

In the ultimate extreme of nihilism, nothing, like all the other things that might be thought to constitute common being, is lost, and so it can only be the loss of nothing that is constitutive of being-in-common.

If nihilism leaves us with the 'with', this might open the way to a less anthropocentric ontology. It is not humanity that is the limit of nihilism, but finitude, and finitude is not shared only by humans. Being singular plural is the condition of all things:

> The difference between humanity and the rest of being . . . does not distinguish true existence from a sort of subexistence. Instead, this difference forms the concrete condition of singularity. We would not be 'humans' if there were not 'dogs' and 'stones'.[36]

What I have in common with a dog or a stone is not being the same being, but finitude is something that everything shares, 'all the dead, all the living, and all beings'.[37]

Losing Touch

Nancy never disguises the fact that being-in-common is a version of Heidegger's account of Being-with (*Mitsein*).[38] Both philosophers see nihilism as turning on the nature of Being-with, but where Heidegger focuses on Being, Nancy concentrates on the 'with', and seeks to distance himself from Heidegger by extending the scope of being singular plural beyond the merely human.

As Heidegger's account of world-poverty makes clear, his account of Being-with cannot accommodate all beings. Being-with belongs 'to the essence of man's existence', and it is for this reason that man cannot be transposed into man. In contrast, man cannot go along with an animal because although animals live with us, and we with them, 'this being-with is not an *existing-with*'.[39] Nancy answers Heidegger's question 'What does this "with" mean?' by saying that the 'with' has no meaning, it is nothing, finitude. On this basis, he suggests that all withs are commensurable. In fact, the 'with' is the 'commensurability of incommensurable singularities' irrespective of whether they originate in 'another person, animal, plant, or star'.[40]

This fails to register Heidegger's insistence that incommensurability is to be found even in the 'with' of finitude. For example, for Nancy death is 'the very signature of the with', because 'it takes place in and through being-with-one-another'.[41] Citing Heidegger, he comments: 'I do not recognize myself in the death of the other . . . I recognize that in the death of the other there is nothing recognizable . . . I experience the other's alterity', and so, for Nancy, 'Community is revealed in the death of others.'[42] But Heidegger argues that death, of its very nature, is a specific and not a universally shared form of finitude: 'To die means to be capable of death as death. Only man dies. The animal perishes.'[43]

Similarly, Nancy emphasises that part of the nature of finitude is that beings must necessarily be in some form of contact with one another, not because they have to border on something, but because 'touch alone exposes the limits at which identities and ipseities can *distinguish themselves* from one another'.[44] In this way

> All of being is in touch with all of being, but the law of touching is separation; moreover it is the heterogeneity of surfaces that touch each other. *Contact* is beyond fullness and emptiness, beyond connection and disconnection.[45]

But it depends, as Heidegger points out, on what is meant by touch:

> The stone is lying on the path, for example. We can say that the stone is exerting a certain pressure on the surface of the earth. It is 'touching' the earth. But what we call 'touching' here is not a form of touching at all in the stronger sense of the word. It is not at all like that relationship which the lizard has to the stone on which it lies basking in the sun. And the touching implied in both these cases is above all not the same as that touch which we experience when we rest our hand upon the head of another human being. The lying upon . . . the touching involved in our three examples is fundamentally different in each case.[46]

Nancy is not necessarily talking about physical touching, but nor is Heidegger. As he acknowledges, 'Taken strictly, "touching" is never what we are talking about in such cases.' No amount of empirical examination can establish whether the chair is touching the wall, because two entities that are themselves worldless can never touch each other.[47]

Heidegger's point that 'when we speak of "Being-with" we always have in view Being with one another in the same world'[48] applies to touching as well. There is no single 'with', no one form of contact, that potentially puts everything in touch with everything else. This does not depend upon stones or lizards lacking particular attributes. The interest of Heidegger's account is not zoological or geological; it is rather that he offers an account of what varying degrees of world-poverty might involve. But if the worldless cannot touch, what about the world-poor? Can they touch, or half-touch? What is given and what is withheld? According to Heidegger, it is the same thing both given and withheld. Hence 'when we say that the lizard is lying on the rock, we ought to cross out the word "rock"'.[49] As Derrida points out, this is the inverse of Being crossed out, where Being is withheld yet given in its withholding.[50] Like Tantalus, the lizard is fated to be both given the rock and to have it snatched away. Its touching will always be a sort of reaching. Or, to put it another way, a form of poverty. Losing touch is one way of losing, of becoming untouchable.

Hearing Noises

There is a similar divergence between Heidegger and Nancy with regard to language. For Nancy, language 'is the *with* as such', the exposition of plural singularity. Before being any particular language, language is the communication that comes with finitude, hence 'communication *is* Being' and 'Being is communication'.[51] Here Nancy echoes Heidegger's view that 'language is not the utterance of an organism . . . [It] is the clearing-concealing advent of Being itself.' But if 'language is the house of Being', then to become world-poor is also to become language-poor. It is because plants and animals are never 'freely placed in the clearing of Being which alone is "world" [that] they lack language'.[52]

According to Nancy, 'Language constitutes itself and articulates itself from out of the "as"'. Without the 'as' there can be no 'with', for the 'with' is just how 'we expose ourselves to one another, *as* "ones" and *as* "others", exposing the world *as* world'.[53] If Chandos's impoverishment involves the loss of the as-structure of the world, the 'language in which mute things speak' cannot be 'the *with* as such'. But in that case it is not silence either. As Heidegger points out, silence presupposes language, so 'to keep silent does not mean to be dumb . . . [for] he who never says anything cannot keep silent at any given moment'.[54] On the contrary, the language that mute things speak is, for Heidegger, only noise. This, at least, is how he describes the calls of animals which are 'merely noises . . . vocal utterances that lack something, namely meaning. The animal does not mean or understand by its call.'[55]

Broch claims that Hofmannsthal's work is infused with 'the dread of the coming silence of humanity'.[56] But although becoming world-poor may mean losing speech, it does not leave the poor to enjoy the silence. Wittgenstein said: 'What we cannot speak about we must pass over in silence.'[57] But that is impossible. Passing over in silence would suggest that you knew the shape and boundaries of that of which you could not speak. In fact, those who cannot speak cannot pass over in silence, for the poor are poor in silence.

Communism Is Music

In 'Myth Interrupted', Nancy rehearses the argument in other terms. On the one hand there is myth: 'Myth communicates the common, the *being-common* of what it reveals or what it recites . . . Myth is always the myth of community, that is to say it is always the myth of a communion.'[58] On the other, there is not language but literature: '"Literature" means the being-in-common of what has no common origin, but is originally in-common or with.'[59] The two are related through interruption:

> When a voice, or music, is suddenly interrupted, one hears just at that instant something else, a mixture of various silences and noises that have been covered over by the sound, but in this something else one hears again the voice or the music that has become in a way the voice or the music of its own interruption: a kind of echo.[60]

'Literature' is the name given to this voice of interruption, when 'in some way the interrupted voice or music imprints the schema of its retreat in the murmur or the rustling to which the interruption gives rise'. Literature therefore functions as an example of the way, in the absence of commonality and communion, that the in-common may constitute itself as a sort of echo. As we write, every text establishes a community, a sort of 'literary communism'. Of course, it is not really even a communism, but it does remind us of one thing: 'we would not write if our being were not shared'.[61]

Nancy's story has, like all myths, been told before—by Nietzsche, in *The Birth of Tragedy*. In Dionysian song and dance, man expresses himself as 'a member of a higher community'. The *principium individuationis* collapses, and 'union between man and man [is] reaffirmed'. The music of Dionysus brings 'universal harmony' in which state and society dissolve and each 'feels himself not only united, reconciled, and fused with his neighbor, but as one with him', as 'the *one* living being'.[62] Indeed, music and tragic myth are both expressions of the Dionysian, 'they are inseparable', for it is only through music that we can understand 'the joy involved in the annihilation of the individual'. In the end 'tragedy perishes with the evanescence of the spirit of music'.[63] This happens when the spirit of science annihilates myth.

> Alas!
> You have shattered
> The beautiful world
> With brazen fist;
> It falls, it is scattered.[64]

For Nietzsche, it was Socrates who had spilled 'the magic potion into the dust'. Now, 'the mythless man stands eternally hungry'.[65]

The genealogy runs from Nietzsche to Nancy: in every case a unity, an immanence, a plenitude, now lost, somehow holds in its absence the promise of presence.[66] Socrates may never have experienced 'frenzy of artistic enthusiasm', yet his influence 'again and again prompts a regeneration of *art*'. Zarathustra proclaims: 'All gods are dead: now we want the Superman to live.' Heidegger's Being 'in staying away . . . promises itself in its unconcealment'. For Nancy, the failure of communism and the retreat of the political 'is the uncovering, the ontological laying bare of being-with'.[67]

But what is the outcome for the unmusical, the unliterary, the uncommunicative? Chandos too had experienced that 'overwhelming feeling of unity leading back to the very heart of nature' to which Nietzsche referred.[68] He describes himself as having formerly been in a constant state of ecstasy, living 'in a kind of continuous inebriation' in which he saw 'all of existence as one great unity . . . I felt nature in all of it . . . and in all of nature I felt myself'. It is this Dionysian unity that disintegrates when Chandos's world falls apart and breaks into pieces.[69]

He, too, becomes deaf to the music, but he does not detect the echo, and only hears the noise. His newfound ecstasies are prompted by 'the stridulation of the last dying cricket . . . not the majestic rumbling of an organ'.[70] Kojève predicted that if man became an animal again, he 'would perform musical concerts after the fashion of frogs and cicadas'.[71] When Chandos takes his place in the audience he finds the concert already in progress. The world-poor, for whom the retreat of Being is not imprinted in the nothing, cannot hear the music, or even the silence. Chandos becomes an unmusical Socrates, a mythless man.

Dies Irae

A single image runs through these texts. The language in which mute things speak to Chandos is, he suggests, also the language 'in which I will perhaps have something to say for myself someday when I am dead and standing before an unknown judge'.[72] It is precisely this act of appearing together on the day of judgement that provides Nancy with his model of being-in-common. On that day, no creature has anything to share with any other, save the fact that all are standing there together: '*In the end* we compear there naked.'[73] This is the moment when, in the words of the *Dies irae*:

> Death benumbs all that emerges
> When creatures rise
> To answer to their judge

As Heidegger notes, 'creatures' here refers to the whole of creation, including man; *all* rise and stand before their judge.[74] The last day is, Agamben observes, the day on which 'relations between animals and men will take on a new form, and . . . man himself will be reconciled with his animal nature'.[75]

The first question of the last day: How did we get here? Taking up Heidegger's theme of the abandonment of being, Nancy suggests that to abandon is, etymologically, to put at *bandon* (a ban or decree). In effect, 'One always abandons to a law'. However, abandonment in this sense is not a summons to appear before any particular court, but to appear before 'the law as such in its totality'.[76] The model for this is the last judgment: 'a simple judgment, without appeal; it is not subject to any superior law for it proceeds from that which precedes law . . . Before this law without law we have never ceased to compear.'[77] Here we are truly abandoned, 'without return and without recourse'.[78]

Agamben picks up Nancy's reading and develops it into an account of abandonment closer to Heidegger's conception of world-poverty. He does this by exploiting the parallels between Heidegger and Schmitt. According to Schmitt, the state of exception is the 'law beyond the law to which we are abandoned', a law that is, in effect, 'no longer a law but a zone of indistinguishability between law and life', while for Heidegger, '*Being is nothing other than the being's being abandoned and remitted to itself . . .* nothing other than the ban of the being.' Agamben uses the analogy to emphasise that 'the relation of abandonment is not a relation'.[79] Just as Being and the being do not part ways but 'remain without relation', so those abandoned to a law maintain themselves 'in relation to something presupposed as nonrelational'.[80]

The implications of this become clearer when Agamben fleshes out the phenomenology of the nonrelation in his various accounts of bare life, the form of life that persists in the state of exception. Bare life is figured by the *Muselmann*, the prisoner in the concentration camps 'who was giving up and was given up by his comrades'. The *Muselmanner* exemplify the impossibility of common being. They 'were so weak; they let themselves do anything. They were people with whom there was no common ground.' But Agamben goes beyond Nancy in emphasising that in this case there was also 'no possibility of communication'.[81] The *Muselmänner* have lost touch, fallen silent, and hear only noises— they are excommunicate, not just in the sense of finding themselves excluded from communion but from communication as well.

To exist in this condition is to become a *homo alalus,* 'neither an animal life nor a human life, but only a life that is separated and excluded from itself—only a *bare life*'.[82] As such, the *Muselmann* is characterised not just by the inability to speak, but by an inability to die. Agamben quotes Heidegger asking rhetorically, 'Do they die? They decease. They are eliminated. They become pieces in the warehouse of the fabrication of corpses.' Disquieting though it is to have the question posed by a former Nazi, Agamben accepts its implication: the *Muselmann* 'is the non-human who obstinately appears as human; he is the human that cannot be told apart from the inhuman'.[83]

As the residuum left when every trace of humanity has been destroyed, the *Muselmann* provides the answer to the question 'What is the "ultimate" sense of belonging to the human species?' Following Primo Levi, Agamben suggests that 'the human being . . . is the one who can survive the human being'.[84] The *Muselmann*'s state is, in Agamben's terms, 'irreparable'. Irreparable means that 'things are consigned without remedy to their being-thus . . . [and] that in their being-thus they are absolutely exposed, absolutely abandoned',[85] just as at the last judgment. Yet if this is so, the fate of the *Muselmann* may be more ambiguous than it appears.

Because the irreparable is 'that things are just as they are', Agamben equates it with the 'yes' of Nietzsche's Superman: 'The yes is said not simply of a state of things, but of its being-*thus*. Only for this reason can it eternally return. The *thus* is eternal.' This is 'the salvation of the profanity of the world, of its being-thus'.[86] But what of those who cannot affirm the eternal return, the lost? Here Agamben cites the Gnostic Basilides, commenting on Paul's Epistle to the Romans, who suggested that after the elect were saved, nature would no longer groan for redemption but be in a 'great ignorance' so that

> in the regions below there will be no news and no knowledge of the realities above, so that the souls below may not be tormented by desiring impossible things, like fish striving to graze on the hills with the sheep—for such a desire would be their destruction.

Agamben notes that in such a case 'natural life that is unsavable and that has been completely abandoned by every spiritual element' is, because of the 'great ignorance', nonetheless 'perfectly blessed'.[87] As a result, after the judgment, 'all the elements and creatures of the world, having completed their theological task . . . enjoy an incorruptible fallenness'.[88] The 'great ignorance' allows both man and animal to 'be outside of being, saved precisely in their being unsavable'.[89]

Where does this leave the *Muselmann*? Such a figure 'is no longer human . . . but if animality had been defined precisely by its poverty in world and by its obscure expectation of a revelation and a salvation, then this life cannot be called animal either'.[90] As the reference to 'poverty in world' makes clear, this is an interpretation conceived in Heideggerian terms. But whereas Heidegger had maintained that the animal's world-poverty made sense of the Pauline text concerning 'the yearning expectation of creatures and creation', Agamben argues that claiming that 'If nature could speak it would lament' makes no sense, for 'nature is messianic precisely because of its eternal and complete caducity'.[91] Redemption is 'the irreparable loss of the lost, the definitive profanity of the profane', which, precisely for this reason, now reaches its limit.[92] Like the fish that does not dream of grazing on the hills, the *Muselmann* exists in his own element with hope of no other. Redeemed by his own hopelessness, he is the human being 'who can survive the human being'.

Agamben's argument here differs significantly from those of Nancy and Heidegger. Whereas Nancy does not acknowledge the possibility of world-poverty, Agamben deliberately excludes it. Nature is not tormented by desiring impossible things, for in the great ignorance, the possibility of any form of transposition is withheld to all. Incorruptible fallenness makes worldless rather than world-poor. Rather than being unsaved and savable, nature is saved because it is unsavable. To be deprived of all humanity is to discover what the human is. Heidegger had suggested that Being is nothing other than the being's being abandoned, but Agamben goes further. By insisting that abandonment is not a relation, he shows that, abandoned by Being, the human being is not human at all.

But this is subhumanism as a humanism, not an antihumanism. Although Agamben, unlike Heidegger, goes beyond the human, he makes the subhuman the locus of his own transcendental argument. Nietzsche had argued that nihilism turns back because devaluation presupposes valuation, and Heidegger that nothing, as the absence of Being, presupposes somewhere that Being might dwell. In both cases this translates into a positive ecology, of the super- over the subhuman, of the human over the animal. Agamben takes the same argument further. Nihilism turns back on itself not in the human, but in the less than human. Like art which 'does not die but, having become a self-annihilating nothing, eternally survives itself',[93] the human survives itself in bare life, for it is only there that the human is laid bare. Rather than being a move in a negative ecology of value, the subhuman is the point at which negation reaches its limit.

The difference between the great ignorance and a negative ecology is clearer still if we turn back to Nietzsche. Nietzsche, too, describes a state like that of the *Muselmann*, calling it the invalid's 'one great means of cure'. It is 'that fatalism without rebellion with which a Russian soldier for whom the campaign has become too much at last lies down in the snow . . . no longer to react at all'. As such it is 'a kind of will to hibernation', which he elsewhere equates with the ascetic's 'attempt to achieve for man something approximating *hibernation* for some kinds of animal . . . the minimum metabolic rate which maintains life below the level of real consciousness'. In effect it is a passive version of the acceptance of the eternal return: 'To accept oneself as a fate, not to desire oneself "different".'[94]

Within Nietzsche's ecology, the irreparable is potentially the basis of a new caste society, the positive ecology of value which alone makes valuation possible. There are the Supermen who accept the eternal return, and the exploited who passively accept their lot 'in the dwarfing and adaptation of man to a specialized utility'.[95] Nietzsche therefore loathes those who threaten the ignorance of the latter. At the end of his paean to the caste system in *The Anti-Christ* he asks: 'Whom among today's rabble do I hate the most? The Socialist rabble, the Chandala apostles who undermine the worker's instinct, his pleasure, his feeling of contentment with his little state of being.' For the mediocre 'it is happiness to be mediocre', and to be 'a public utility, a cog . . . is a natural vocation'.[96]

Although bare life might potentially be part of a negative ecology, it can also be redeemed, either by absorption into a caste society and a positive ecology, or by being detotalised so that there is no longer an ecology and all are trapped in blissful ignorance. In the latter case, individuals inhabit worlds that are discrete, whereas in world-poverty they are captivated by fragments of the one world they all share. In the great ignorance all are happy in their own worlds, whereas the world-poor, like Tolstoy's unhappy families, are all deprived of the same thing in different ways.

Worldless Worlds

Through what mechanisms might such poverty come about? How is world at the same time both given and taken away? Heidegger offers two related accounts of the process—world-poverty and world-darkening—and one may offer some insight into the other. The darkening of the world is always the darkening of *spiritual* world, and as such it involves a disempowering and misinterpretation of spirit in which the spiritual is instrumentalised and divided up into regions each with its own standards. This can be seen in the division of intellectual labour in the sciences and is an omen of the darkening that is 'the onslaught of what we call the demonic'.[97]

Heidegger's equation of the darkening of the world with scientific specialisation is in line with the concerns of nineteenth-century sociologists from Comte onwards. Some, however, viewed the prospect with more equanimity. While accepting that 'individual minds . . . are finite and none can work from all points of view at once', Durkheim argues that each of these points of view represent 'separate tasks within the joint enterprise' and form partial truths that come together in the collective consciousness. This is consciousness formed not by 'uniting to form a single collective mind', but by 'communicating in one object which is the same for all'. Individual minds, 'like Leibniz's monads', each can then give expression to 'the entirety of the universe' from their own point of view.[98]

Durkheim interpreted scientific specialisation in terms of the wider division of labour which meant that as society becomes more complex, it is impossible for it to maintain a single sense of itself.[99] When this happens, collective sentiments become progressively less able to contain the centrifugal tendencies of specialisation.[100] It is, however, only in the case of an anomic division of labour that the 'disconnected parts . . . fail to co-operate with one another'. In normal circumstances, being 'adjacent to one another' they are in sufficient contact to have a 'continuous feeling of their mutual dependence', and to adjust to changes to maintain equilibrium. Only if contacts become rare do the parts become 'too distant from one another to be aware of all the bonds that unite them'.[101] Then the individual, bent low over his task like a workman making pinheads, 'will no longer be aware of the collaborators who work at his side . . . no longer [have] any idea at all of what that common task consists.'[102]

According to Nancy, there are two ways of fulfilling (and so destroying) the with: 'filling it up, or emptying it out'. Either way, being ceases to be singular and plural. In the former, the singular is subsumed within the totality, in the latter 'the singular exists on its own and, therefore, as a totality'.[103] If the one is a 'single collective mind', the other is a form of monadology. This is the fate of the world-poor. Losing touch with one another, they find their world becoming increasingly anomic, 'an abyss of intransitivity'. Each says nothing in a way that others cannot understand. With what result? Leibniz famously likened the pre-established harmony of his window-less monads to an orchestra where (in the words of Michel Serres):

> Each musician plays his instrument as if he were alone in the world. He likes only his English horn, this English horn is he himself in person. He plays his part of the score, and when he has finished, at the very end of the page, he puts down his things and leaves the theatre.[104]

For the excommunicate, however, there is no music and no pre-established harmony: 'the collective is white noise itself', or perhaps white silence.[105] But unlike the great ignorance, where the collective task is finished and every sphere echoes with its own music, each monad is, thanks to the division of labour, unknowingly part of a single orchestra. Even the *Muselmann* can play a rest in the cacophony of the world.

But no one notices, for all are preoccupied with their own activities, their worlds not only windowless but barely commensurable. As Heidegger explains, 'The blade of grass that the beetle crawls up, for example, is not a blade of grass for it at all; it is not something possibly destined to become part of a bundle of hay with which the peasant will feed his cow. The blade of grass is simply a beetle-path on which the beetle specifically seeks beetle-nourishment.'[106] This very incommensurability is, however, what permits the coexistence of existences of different kinds. It is precisely because they do not touch that they do not come into conflict. When Durkheim described an oak tree on which could be found two hundred species of insects that had no contact with one another, it was a profusion made possible by the fact that 'Some feed on the fruits of the tree, others on leaves, yet more on bark and roots.'[107] Each one ignores the others because it is captivated by different things.

Lukács claimed that the Chandos letter expressed, more clearly than any tragedy, the fragmentation of contemporary life; and now, perhaps, it is possible to see why. Chandos's terrifying experience enacts within the compass of a single life the entire social transformation described by modernity. He had once seen all of existence as one great unity, but gradually, beginning with the most abstract and general notions, everything becomes meaningless to him, except seemingly trivial and random objects. Like Durkheim's workman with his pinhead, Chandos becomes focused on just one point and no longer connects with anything else. When he ignores his tenants standing respectfully outside their doors and finds his gaze passing through them in search of 'that one whose unprepossessing form . . . whose mute existence can become the source of that mysterious, wordless, infinite rapture',[108] he is

Heidegger's beetle on its beetle path, one of Durkheim's insects seeking its nourishment. He is discovering how to live in a complex society.

The alignment of Durkheim and Heidegger here owes something to their shared debt to Leibniz, whose monadology provides a model not only for Durkheim's account of specialisation, but for Heidegger's account of captivation as well.[109] But it is more than that. If to become poor in world is to become poor in common consciousness, Heidegger's attempt to exempt the human from the world-poverty of the animal is inextricably entwined with the desire to release humanity from the world-darkening of modernity. No wonder he uses the metaphor of darkness to describe both states. Nature provides us with a model of what social interaction is like without common consciousness. Becoming animal is becoming modern, perhaps, as Kojève suggests, the future of modernity. A negative ecology of value must eventually involve participating in a division of labour broader than a merely economic one, an ontological division of labour, a being plural plural. That is what an ecology is. Becoming world-poor opens up the possibility for a degree of anomie beyond that possible within purely human interaction. You cannot fully experience anomie within the species; you have to go outside. The human world is never dark enough.

6

Counter-Interest

The dream of the mountaineer . . . effortless falling.

Nietzsche

He dreams repeatedly of the same thing: 'the pleasure found of falling in the dust, the peace of happiness in misfortune', the pleasure of dreaming oneself 'a child, beggar and fool'.[1] It is a symptom of the will to power: those who seek after power fall asleep and dream of the opposite course: 'Suddenly and deeply to sink into a feeling as into a whirlpool . . . For once quite without power . . . *powerlessness*'. But it is also the opposite of the will to power in that it is an *unwilled* powerlessness, an 'effortless falling as though by the pull of gravity'. Nietzsche presents the dream as a necessary release after which 'one is again freer, more refreshed, colder, more severe, and again resumes one's unwearying quest for its opposite: for *power*'.[2] And yet it must be more than that, for unwilled powerlessness is the unspoken presupposition of all will to power, and if will to power knows no limit, neither does its opposite.

Like Nietzsche, a wanderer and a mountain climber, Zarathustra has a vision of himself ascending a solitary mountain path with a dwarf perched on his shoulder. The dwarf is his devil and archenemy, 'the Spirit of Gravity'. Zarathustra struggles on, despite the spirit trying to draw him down toward the abyss; 'O Zarathustra', the dwarf says mockingly, each syllable like a drop of lead poured into his ear, 'you stone of wisdom! You have thrown yourself high, but every stone that is thrown must—fall!'³ The scene echoes the prologue, where Zarathustra watches a tightrope walker walking across a rope stretched between two towers over a market square. When a buffoon comes up behind him and jumps over him, the tightrope walker loses his balance, throws away his pole, and falls.⁴

Nietzsche sometimes imagines a falling free of gravity. The madman who proclaims the death of God asks: 'Are we not perpetually falling? Backward, sideward, forward, in all directions? Is there still any up or down? Are we not straying as though through an infinite nothing?'⁵ Falling like this is more like flying, 'a certain divine frivolity, an "upward" without tension and constraint, a "downward" without condescension and humiliation'.⁶ And with gravity? The tightrope walker falls, faster even than his pole, 'a vortex of legs and arms', crashing to the ground in the middle of the square.

'Man', Zarathustra says, 'is a rope, fastened between animal and Superman.' He falls because, as Nietzsche explains in the *Genealogy of Morals*, he 'who believed himself almost a god' has become 'an animal, an animal in the literal sense'.⁷ As the dying tightrope walker tells Zarathustra, he is no more than 'an animal . . . taught to dance by blows and starvation'. With gravity, man does not stray through an infinite nothing; he falls toward it: 'he rolls faster and faster away from the centre—in what direction? Towards nothingness?'⁸ How far is it possible to fall? We cannot tell. The animal is the nothingness that we can see.

Ascent and Descent

Nietzsche distinguishes between 'a type of ascending life and another type of decay, disintegration, weakness'.⁹ The difference between the two is fundamental: 'Every individual may be regarded as representing the ascending or descending line of life.'¹⁰ Which one it is will be of decisive importance for the individual's social value:

If he represents the ascending course of mankind, then his value is in fact extraordinary; and extreme care may be taken over the preservation and promotion of his development . . . if he represents the descending course, decay, chronic sickening, then he has little value: and the first demand of fairness is for him to take as little space, force, and sunshine as possible from the well-constituted.[11]

The diverging trajectories of ascent and descent presuppose the fundamental distinction between strength and weakness, with which they are naturally, though not always historically, coterminous. But what is strength and what is weakness? In the first instance a set of inherited qualities, which Nietzsche sometimes expresses in terms of racial or species difference.[12] These qualities are both physical and mental.[13] In physical terms 'a powerful physicality, a rich, burgeoning, even overflowing health';[14] in psychic terms, a strength that is more difficult to define (it is, in a sense, Nietzsche's life's work to do so) but would include will to power (that is, the will to give strength its natural expression), resistance to suffering, and immunity to pity—all qualities implied by acceptance of the eternal return.

These inherited differences are the cause of a particular type of relationship in which the strong either devour or enslave the weak. The former is exemplified by the relation of predator to prey, the latter by that of master and slave. In the natural order of things, 'men of prey . . . still in possession of unbroken strength of will and lust for power, hurled themselves upon weaker, more civilized, more peaceful races'.[15] This sort of asymmetrical relationship is, Nietzsche argues, not just the result of disparities in physical and mental strength, but actually necessary to their existence: 'Life itself is *essentially* appropriation, injury, overpowering of what is alien and weaker.'[16] To be mentally strong, 'to love, as we do, danger, war, and adventures, [to] refuse to compromise, to be captured, reconciled and castrated', is also inevitably to 'think about the necessity for new orders, also for a new slavery—for

every strengthening and enhancement of the human type also
involves a new kind of enslavement'.[17]

According to Nietzsche this is the form that ascent and descent
naturally takes; indeed it is not entirely clear whether it is meaningful to speak of strength and weakness independently of one
another, for these are relative terms.[18] People are strong or weak
relative to one another's strength or weakness, and what defines
that strength or weakness is the competitive advantage it provides
in any possible combat or contest (the Greek *agon*), even if such
combat has not yet taken place. Human society is not a contract
but an experiment, an experiment designed to discover who can
command and who can obey.[19]

However, Nietzsche's accounts of ascent and descent also
invoke another dichotomy, that of sickness and health. This over-
laps with that between strength and weakness, insofar as the
healthy are naturally stronger than the sick. Nietzsche frequently
refers to 'the sick and the weak' as though they were the same
thing. But he also sometimes separates the two, though when he
does so his claims are contradictory. On the one hand he argues
that, through inheritance, each individual represents not just
himself but his entire lineage 'up to and including himself', and
that sickness is therefore the consequence of a descending trajectory 'already a phenomenon consequent upon decay, *not* the cause
of it'.[20] On the other hand, he points to historical examples in which
making others sick was the means through which they were weakened. In ancient India, he suggests, the Laws of Manu prescribed
an inadequate diet and hygiene for the untouchables, in order to
make them sick, and thus 'weak and harmless'.[21] And in medieval
Europe, the Teutons, the 'blond beasts', were made sick by the
Christian Church in order to tame them: 'In physiological terms:
in the struggle with the [blond] beast, making it sick *can* be the
only means of making it weak.'[22]

The latter example demonstrates the ambiguous nature of sickness, for sickness does not afflict only the weak. Sickness may be

primarily associated with a descending trajectory, but it can also cross over to the ascending one. In order for some to grow healthy and strong, others have to become sick and weak, but this creates a new hazard potentially capable of reversing those dynamics: the sick can infect the healthy and weaken them in their turn:

> The sick represent the greatest danger for the healthy; it is *not* the strongest but the weakest who spell disaster for the strong . . . The *sickly* constitute the greatest danger to man: *not* the evil, *not* the 'predators'. Those who are from the outset victims, downtrodden, broken—they are the ones, the *weakest* are the ones who must undermine life amongst men.[23]

How does this happen?

The Dialectic of the Sick

To be weak and sick results in suffering; indeed, simply to be on a descending trajectory is itself a form of suffering. Nietzsche takes it for granted that, given the agonistic nature of life, the majority are on such a trajectory and suffer necessarily.[24] The primary relationship life offers is having power over or being disempowered, causing or experiencing suffering. But the story does not end there, for there is potentially a different kind of relationship, secondary to the first, based on compassion. To feel pity, *Mitleid,* is to suffer with, literally to feel com-passion. This too is an asymmetrical relationship, and it is felt primarily, but not exclusively, by the strong for the weak. Being strong causes others to be weak, and thus to suffer. Compassion creates the possibility that the strong, who necessarily cause suffering, may through compassion end up sharing in the suffering that they themselves have created.

It takes Nietzsche some time to settle on this paradoxical

conclusion. He is always critical of the idea that compassion is in itself a virtue, but he explores the theme from a variety of angles. In *The Gay Science* he advances the idea that pity, rather than compensating the weak for their domination by the strong, is actually one of the routes through which that domination is exercised:

> When we see somebody suffer, we like to exploit this opportunity to take possession of him; those who become his benefactors and pity him, for example, do this and call the lust for a new possession that he awakens in them 'love'; and the pleasure they feel is comparable to that aroused by the prospect of a new conquest.[25]

On this view, compassion never evades the logic of power even for a moment. Pity is just 'an agreeable impulse of the instinct for appropriation at the sight of what is weaker', and benefiting others is just as much a way of exercising power over them as hurting them.[26] The only difference is that the former requires less strength. Nietzsche therefore suggests that 'Pity is the most agreeable feeling amongst those who have little pride and no prospects of great conquests; for them easy prey—and that is what all who suffer are—is enchanting.'[27]

Later, however, Nietzsche comes to realise that compassion is also potentially a way in which power can be exercised by the weak over the strong. He emphatically rejects Schopenhauer's understanding of empathy as a 'mystical process by virtue of which *pity* makes two beings into one and in this way makes possible the immediate understanding of the one by the other',[28] but nevertheless acknowledges that empathy involves imitating the feelings of another in ourselves. To feel compassion for the suffering is therefore to imitate their suffering in ourselves and suffer as they do.

Described like this, Nietzsche's account of compassion appears to function rather like Hegel's master-slave dialectic, save that the struggle for existence is transposed from the battlefield to the sanitorium. Sickness is both the product of weakness and produced by it. The healthy strong overcome the weak and sick, but compassion allows the weak to overcome the strong by infecting them with their sickness. Then the trajectories are reversed. The consciousness of the sick becomes that of the strong, weakening them relative to the weak, who become stronger by comparison.

Nietzsche therefore argues that pity has two negative consequences. First, it enhances the power of the weak over the strong, because inciting pity is a way for the weak to make the strong suffer too. Making someone else suffer consoles sufferers by revealing that 'despite all their weakness, they still have at least one *power: the power to hurt*'.[29] Second, it serves to increase the amount of suffering in the world. Thanks to pity, it is not just the weak who suffer, as they necessarily must, but also the strong who now unnecessarily suffer with them. Hence Nietzsche's claim that 'pity is an infection' in which 'the suffering of others infects us'.[30] The result is that 'The loss of force which life has already sustained through suffering is increased and multiplied even further', bringing about 'a collective loss of life and life-energy'.[31]

Such collective loss occurs not only because the strong suffer as well as the weak, but because compassion induces the strong to spare the weak and so augment the amount of suffering in the world. It thus 'thwarts the law of evolution . . . it defends life's disinherited and condemned; [and] through the abundance of the ill-constituted of all kinds which it retains in life . . . gives life itself a gloomy and questionable aspect'.[32] This is why Nietzsche thinks the morality of compassion inevitably leads to nihilism: 'Pity is practical nihilism . . . [Both] as a multiplier of misery and as a conservator of everything miserable . . . pity persuades to nothingness.'[33]

Undialectical Sickness

If, as this implies, compassion is a route to a negative ecology of value, does this mean that reading like a loser can be identified with pity? Reading like a loser is interpreting the world to one's own disadvantage, so that the interpretation results in loss to the interpreter. But what is the relationship between reading in such a way that one becomes a loser and the interpretation of others' loss—in other words, between the primary movement of ascent/ descent and the secondary one produced by compassion?

Within Nietzsche's scheme, pity, or the lack of it, does not necessarily have the same effect on all who experience it. In particular, it has a different value and performs a different function within the lives of the strong and the weak. The primary focus of Nietzsche's writing on pity is the compassionate strong, both because pity is more likely to be felt by the strong for the weak, and because such pity is likely to have some effect: 'A man who is by nature a *master*—when such a man has pity, well, *this* pity has value. But what good is the pity of those who suffer. Or those who, worse, *preach* pity.'[34]

Nietzsche has particular targets in mind when he refers to the *compassionate strong*—above all, Schopenhauer and Pascal.[35] Such men are directly afflicted by the suffering of the weak as a result of compassion, and by adopting the morality of pity they also undermine their own strength. Although compassion does not unite the strong with the weak, it effectively doubles the ego by seeing things from someone else's point of view, creating a division of the self in which one side is sacrificed for the other.[36] When this happens, everything that distinguishes the strong from the weak 'enters their consciousness accompanied by a feeling of diminution and discredit'. The result is that strength itself becomes the source of 'the inner enfeeblement, discouragement, self-vexation of the non-herd animals'.[37]

If for the strong pity is a form of ascetic self-denial, for the *compassionate weak* it is a form of disguised self-assertion. This can happen in a variety of ways. To have the reassurance that others are suffering as they do is, Nietzsche suggests, the reason why the weak both offer and accept pity: man is dissatisfied with himself, 'he suffers—and his vanity wants him to suffer only with others, to feel pity'.[38] Because they are weak, the sick have very little to offer each other directly except sympathy itself—hence Nietzsche's question: 'what good is the pity of those who suffer?'[39] However, they have much to gain from the creation of an ideology that promotes pity and the abolition of suffering as communal goals. The weak then assert themselves by arguing that this form of weakness is actually the greatest of virtues. In the slave morality, 'those qualities are brought out and flooded with light which serve to ease existence for those who suffer . . . pity, the complaisant and obliging hand, the warm heart, patience, industry, humility, and friendliness'.[40]

When the strong accept this ideology, they seek to preserve the weak and alleviate their suffering. The strong themselves become weaker in the process, improving not only the comparative but also the relative position of the weak. Arousing the compassion of the strong is for the weak a means of exercising power, something, Nietzsche claims, that women long ago discovered in their relations with men. Women rule when, conspiring with 'the types of decadence, the priests, against the "powerful", the "strong", the men', they succeed in overcoming the strong.[41] The priests, represented by the figure of the 'ascetic priest' in the *Genealogy of Morals*, are 'physicians and nurses *who are themselves sick*'.[42] It is hard to tell whether they are examples of the compassionate strong grown sick, or of the compassionate weak grown strong, for they are the creation of the dialectic between the two.

Against this ethical model, Nietzsche extols the virtues of the *uncompassionate strong*, the 'noble and courageous' man who 'is actually proud of the fact that he is *not* made for pity'. Such men might help the unfortunate out of an urge 'begotten by excess of power', but they nevertheless maintain 'a slight disdain and caution regarding compassionate feelings'.[43] Insofar as they experience it, the pity of the uncompassionate strong is directed not towards the weak, but rather towards the compassionate strong who waste their strength in pity for the weak. What Nietzsche calls '*My kind*

of "pity"' is the feeling produced by the sight of 'precious capabili-
ties squandered', not pity for the sick and unfortunate members of
society. [44] But in having pity for the pitier rather than the pitied, it
is not the weakness of the pitier that is pitied, but rather the waste
of creative strength. This is, as Nietzsche says, 'pity *versus* pity', a
pity that never engages with the weak or with weakness itself.

Far from feeling compassion for the suffering of the weak, the
uncompassionate take strong delight in it:[45] 'You want, if possible—and there is no more insane "if possible"—*to abolish suffering.*
And we? It really seems that *we* would rather have it higher and
worse than ever . . .'[46] Without compassion, the secondary connec-
tion between those on rising and falling trajectories is broken, and
all follow their own destinies. As Zarathustra explains, the objective of the uncompassionate strong is to enhance rather than
diminish the gap between ascent and descent:

> O my brothers, am I then cruel? But I say: That which is falling
> should also be pushed! Everything of today—it is falling, it is
> decaying? But I—want to push it too! Do you know the delight
> that rolls stones into precipitous depths . . .
>   And him you do not teach to fly, teach—*to fall faster!*'[47]

The category to which Nietzsche gives least attention is that of
the *uncompassionate weak*. Provided the strong remain indifferent
to both to their suffering and their morality, Nietzsche is content
for the weak themselves to remain compassionate, pacifying one
another with the platitudes of the herd morality. However, in
Daybreak he contrasts the tradition in which 'Pity becomes the
antidote to self-destruction' with that of the savage who neither
seeks nor offers pity, considering the former to be humiliating and
the latter contemptible.[48] Nietzsche imagines the savage as the
victor in combat who would let his opponent go free if he sought
mercy, not out of compassion, but out of contempt at his unworthi-
ness. Although he does not draw the analogy, the implication is

that if in the same situation the savage himself were the weaker he would not seek mercy and would be killed.

This, of course, would not preclude the possibility that, if the opponent of the savage weak were one of the compassionate strong, the savage might, by virtue of being weak, arouse the pity of the strong and be spared. The savage weak may still undermine the strong by becoming the objects of pity, but they do not feel pity for each other or promote the morality of compassion. In consequence, the dialectical relationship between the compassionate weak (seeking pity) and the compassionate strong (giving pity) is broken. Lacking the antidote to self-destruction, the savage weak are the weak who do not conquer.

Interpreted like this, the countervailing dynamics of Nietzsche's dialectical system are domination and contagion. Ascent is achieved either through domination or through spreading contagion; descent involves either being dominated yourself or being contaminated by others who are. Compassion is the vector of contagion, and as such it does not have the same effect on all: the compassionate strong reach down to those who are descending, and are dragged down in their turn, while the compassionate weak reach up to break their fall. Reading like a loser means compassion for the less fortunate only when it is itself a becoming less fortunate. It is the trajectory of the compassionate strong and of the savage weak.

Counter-Interest

How then does reading like a loser diverge from the morality of Schopenhauer? It differs not only in its inclusion of the unmediated failure of the savage weak, but also in its interpretation of the compassion of the strong. Schopenhauer's account of compassion is a distinctive one. It starts from the observation of nature and the ceaseless processes of change and movement that drive plants and animals through life towards death. This biological observation furnishes the basic elements of his philosophical system: 'We have long since recognized this striving, that constitutes the kernel and in-itself of everything, as the same thing that in us . . . is called will. We call its hindrance through an obstacle placed between it and its temporary goal, suffering.'[49]

Both will and the suffering that arises from its inevitable frustration are omnipresent and seemingly inescapable. Surveying this spectacle the observer cannot help but feel some sympathy for those involved in it. However, as Schopenhauer follows Rousseau in pointing out, 'direct sympathy with another is restricted to his *suffering*. It is not roused, at any rate not directly, by his *well-being*.' Sympathy or compassion is the 'immediate participation, independent of all ulterior considerations, primarily in the suffering of another, and thus in the prevention or elimination of it'.[50]

The effect of this is to take the interests of others to heart so that they are no longer something external to the observer, but something that is experienced directly in the same way (but, Schopenhauer acknowledges, not always to the same degree) as the observer's own sufferings and triumphs:

> I suffer directly with him, I feel *his* woe just as I ordinarily feel only my woe; and, likewise, I directly desire his weal in the same way I otherwise desire only my own. But this requires that I am in some way *identified with him*, in other words, that this entire *difference* between me and everyone else, which is the very basis of my egoism, is eliminated, to a certain extent at least.[51]

Compassion is not an exclusive relationship between one person and another, but rather something that one person might feel for many others (or many for one). In Schopenhauer's account, it does not so much lead to the abolition of difference between one individual and another as to the abolition of difference between all humans, indeed, all beings. And if someone no longer makes a distinction between himself and others, 'he must also regard the endless sufferings of all that lives as his own, and take upon himself the pain of the whole world'.[52]

It is when 'no suffering is any longer strange or foreign to him. . . . [and] everything lies equally near to him' that man 'sees through the *principium individuationis*' and 'the identity of the will in all its phenomena' becomes apparent.[53] According to Schopenhauer, the inevitable result of this experience of the universality of the will is the denial of the individual will, for if 'the individuality and fate of others are treated entirely like one's own . . . no reason exists for preferring another's individuality to one's own'. To will one's own advantage at the expense of another's would be self-contradictory. As a consequence:

> The will now turns away from life; it shudders from the pleasures in which it recognizes the affirmation of life. Man attains to the state of voluntary renunciation, resignation, true composure and complete will-lessness.

This, Schopenhauer suggests, is the state prefigured in aesthetic contemplation when 'we are raised for the moment above all willing'.[54]

The final move in this argument provides the basis for Nietzsche's critique. Schopenhauer claims that when knowledge is snatched from the thraldom of the will 'it considers things without interest'.[55] Nietzsche, in contrast, emphasises the impossibility of disinterest in both ethics and aesthetics, insisting that 'the whole morality of self-denial . . . no less than the aesthetics of "contemplation devoid of interest"' must be mercilessly questioned. His suspicion that 'the "disinterested" action is an *exceedingly* interesting and interested action' forms the basis of his critique of Schopenhauer's underlying Kantianism.[56] He is scornful of Schopenhauer's suggestion that Kant's definition of the beautiful as 'That which pleases *without interest*' might be the model of disinterested contemplation.

Referring to Schopenhauer's almost obsessive concern with sexual desire, Nietzsche asks:

> Might one not ultimately raise the objection that Schopenhauer was extremely mistaken to think himself a Kantian in this respect . . . that the pleasure of the beautiful was for him too one of 'interest', even one of the very strongest, most personal interest: that of the tortured man who is freed from his torture?[57]

The implication here is that it might actually be a form of interest to be released from interest or desire. Nietzsche asks, 'what does it mean when a philosopher praises the ascetic ideal?—we receive here at least a first hint: he wishes to be *freed from a form of torture*'.[58] According to Schopenhauer the denial of the will is an attempt to stop causing suffering, because through compassion the agent experiences the reality of the suffering his will might cause. But Nietzsche cleverly switches this around. Rather than being an altruistic attempt to prevent the suffering of others, denial of the will is actually an attempt to free oneself of the suffering experienced as a result of compassion.

This argument, too, can be read in terms of the master-slave dialectic. For Schopenhauer compassion leads to identification with others and thus the experience of the universality of humanity and so to the renunciation of self as opposed to other in recognition of the shared identity of both. But where Hegel had argued that for the slave the experience of universal self-consciousness was the first step towards emancipation, Schopenhauer shifts the emphasis to the master, who having recognised the will as universal, emancipates himself from it. Nietzsche, on the other hand, emphasises (like Hegel) that for the master the experience of universal consciousness is a form of double consciousness which must involve experience of the slave in himself, and so infection with the very sickness that weakened the slave in the first place. In this context, renunciation of the will is an attempt at disengagement, an attempt to avoid sickness and to expel the slave consciousness. Nietzsche has an alternative solution: avoid compassion in the first place. Once the contagion has spread, the sickness may be impossible to cure.

In Nietzsche's account there is no escape from interest; we are always willing, valuing, even as we devalue, will nothingness, or contemplate with disinterest. We are always reading for victory. Is there a way to read like a loser that is not a form of disguised self-interest? Paradoxically, Schopenhauer himself provides an example. Compassion, according to Schopenhauer, means sharing the suffering of the other, turning the fate of the other against oneself. Here, the other is the loser through whom reading passes, so that one loses oneself. Renunciation of the will is the means through which the experience of losing is terminated. As one of the compassionate strong, Schopenhauer is reading like a loser, interpreting the world against his own interest; if he is disinterested he is reading for victory.

Soft

For Nietzsche, will is a form of interest and so is its denial. Counter-interest therefore takes the form not of the denial of the will but of weakness of the will. This is already apparent in Nietzsche's characterisation of Schopenhauer. Denial of the will, and the attempt to find something 'valuable in willing no more, in "being a subject *without* aim and purpose"', is, he suggests, the 'great symptom of the *exhaustion* or the *weakness* of the *will*'.[59] In other words, denial of the will is not itself weakness of the will, but the response to it, designed to bring an end to the suffering that weakness causes.

But what is will? Nietzsche claims that Schopenhauer is subject to a fundamental misunderstanding in treating the will as though it were essentially 'craving, instinct, drive'.[60] And it is true that Schopenhauer frequently equates the will and the passions and treats compassion as a countervailing passion, through which the will is quietened.[61] Nietzsche, in contrast, argues that the will is that which masters cravings.[62] But although he claims that weakness of will is a failure to control the passions or drives, he also insists that weakness of the will is a misleading concept, arguing that 'there is no will, and consequently neither a strong nor a weak will'.[63] Rather than a single or universal will, there are merely quanta of will struggling to conquer each other.[64] The two accounts might appear to be contradictory, but they are not, for Nietzsche does not consider the will that masters the drives to be essentially different in kind to the drives that are mastered: 'The multitude and disaggregation of impulses and the lack of any systematic order amongst them result in a "weak will"; their coordination under a single predominant impulse results in a "strong will"'.[65] Will is merely the dominant drive, and if it, in turn, is mastered by another drive, then the will as such is no weaker. Weakness appears only in the disaggregation that results from the absence of mastery.

One cause of such disaggregation, and so of the weakness of the will, is 'the inability *not* to react to a stimulus', which, Nietzsche claims, is itself 'merely another form of degeneration'.[66] His particular focus is compassion, which he interprets as 'a special case of the inability to withstand stimuli', a form of weakness 'like every losing of oneself through a harmful affect'.[67] Within this context, compassion functions not so much as a potentially dominant impulse itself, but rather as one that undermines the mastery of a single predominant impulse and produces a multiplication that undermines unity.

The idea that weakness of will is an inability to withstand stimuli is ultimately derived from Aristotle's discussion of *akrasia*. Aristotle distinguished between two dispositions which, in relation to the stimulus of pleasure, are characterised as unrestraint (*akrasia*) and restraint, and in relation to that of pain, as softness and endurance.[68] Nietzsche extols endurance and restraint, and the interplay of hard and soft becomes one of his most characteristic tropes. His ideal of the noble human being is someone 'who has power over himself . . . who delights in being severe and hard with himself and respects all severity and hardness'. Zarathustra repeatedly exhorts his followers to harden themselves: 'Only the noblest is perfectly hard. This new law-table do I put over you, O my brothers: *Become hard*.' [69]

On the other side, Nietzsche is less concerned with the unrestraint that comes from an inability to withstand pleasurable stimuli as with the softness that comes from an inability to withstand pain, either one's own or that of others. The history of nihilism is therefore the history of softening, and Nietzsche has a rich vocabulary to describe it. Christianity conquered through 'extreme mildness, sweetness, softness'. As a result, the last millennium has seen an 'undeniable softening, humanizing, mellowing of the European', furthered by Rousseau's 'softening, weakening, [and] moralization of man'.[70] Nothing is now 'as timely as weakness of the will'. [71] Eventually, Nietzsche suggests, there comes 'a point in the history of society when it becomes so pathologically soft and tender that . . . it sides even with those who harm it'.[72]

Aristotle associates *akrasia* with impetuosity and softness with inertia, like that of the man who 'lets his cloak trail on the ground to escape the fatigue and trouble of lifting it'. According to Nietzsche, it is inertia of this kind that is presupposed and fostered by nihilism. Suggesting that 'The prime concern of all great religions is the struggle against a certain fatigue and inertia which has grown to epidemic proportions', he argues that rather than going against the grain of inertia, nihilistic religions have gone with it: 'This domineering listlessness is combated through means which reduce the feeling of life itself to its lowest point.'[73] This, according to Nietzsche, is the response of the Buddha, and of Schopenhauer himself. But rather than denying the self, 'in the teaching of Buddha egoism becomes a duty: the "one thing needful", the "how can *you* get rid of suffering" '.[74] For Schopenhauer too, denial of the will does not further weaken the will, but rather reasserts it. As

Nietzsche here implies (but does not seem to notice), when inertia becomes a goal, it is no longer truly akratic, no longer, in fact, a form of inertia at all.

In Nietzsche's own terms, inertia refers to the weakness of will that arises from the failure of one impulse to dominate the others. As such it is the source of the virtues of herd morality, of truthfulness ('which causes us the minimum of spiritual effort') and sympathy ('something passive compared with the activity that maintains and constantly practices the individual's rights to value judgments'). Hence he argues that 'All good people are weak . . . good because they are not strong enough to be evil.' Nietzsche attributes the sentiment to a Latuka chieftain, but he could also have read it in La Rochefoucauld: 'Nobody deserves to be praised for goodness unless he is strong enough to be bad, for any other goodness is usually merely inertia or lack of will.'[75]

There is a homology here between the microcosm of the individual and the macrocosm of the social. Both are composed of a multitude of competing interests, the individual of a multitude of competing drives or points of will, society by a multitude of competing individuals, each of whom may or may not have a dominant interest that disciplines the others. When the individual's drives are subordinated to one master, the individual is strong, and potentially strong enough to subordinate other individuals (one dominant drive in effect subordinating the drives of multiple individuals). When the individual's interests are disaggregated, 'a cosmopolitan chaos of affects and intelligences' like the European of the future, the individual is weak, open to subordination by stronger individuals, but also potentially the cause of social weakness due to an excess of individuals unable to dominate one another. To be soft is to be disaggregated like sand, both within the individual and as individuals, each grain a point of will augmenting or losing its power, but unable to fight its way up out of the chaos to give it form.[76]

In this way, the akratic behaviour of individuals 'whose will is weak, who know what on balance ought to be done, but have insufficient grit, or application, or nerve, or will power, to do it'[77] feeds inexorably into the social entropy that Nietzsche calls the history of nihilism. For Nietzsche, as for Sartre, 'the *soft* is . . . an annihilation which is stopped half way'.[78]

Weakness and Interpretation

If, for Nietzsche, weakness of will does not involve willing something weak, or even willing something weakly, but willing something unsuccessfully through weakness, then it is not easily accommodated within 'weak thought' as it is understood by Gianni Vattimo. For Vattimo, whose account of nihilism presupposes that of Nietzsche and Heidegger, weak thought is not an inability to think (of the kind that might exist because we are distracted, unable to concentrate, or feeble-minded) but rather a form of thinking that is itself weak in the sense that it asserts only what is limited, or is limited in its assertion. On his reading, the hermeneutic ideal represented by Nietzsche's 'There are no facts, only interpretations; and this too is an interpretation' implies both. [79]

Understanding weakness this way has implications for the history of nihilism, where Vattimo follows the 'left Heideggerian' approach that construes 'the history of Being as the story of a "long goodbye" . . . in which Being asymptotically consumes itself, dissolves, grows weak'.[80] For him, there is no question of remembering Being by making it present again, only of remembering the oblivion, and so 'recognising the link between the interpretative essence of truth and nihilism'. Nihilism avoids the 'return of Being' in the acknowledgement that its interpretation of the weakening of Being is itself part of that weakening.[81] In other words, it acknowledges both that the meaning of Being 'is the dissolution of the principle of reality into the manifold of interpretations'[82] and that this acknowledgement is itself one of the manifold of interpretations into which Being has dissolved. Hence, hermeneutics is both the accomplishment of, and an emancipation from, nihilism.

Vattimo claims that acknowledging that an interpretation is only an interpretation constitutes the 'moderation' of the strong to which Nietzsche refers in the Lenzer Heide fragment:

> Nietzschean nihilistic moderation is . . . an ideal of life and wisdom that ultimately sees the goal of moral refinement as a 'plural' subject capable of living his/her own interpretation of the world without needing to believe that it is 'true' in the metaphysical sense of the word.[83]

To do this, he suggests, means 'overcoming the instinct within oneself for preservation, one's interest in the struggle for existence'.[84] The unavoidable implication is therefore that the Superman is he who has overcome his interest in the struggle for existence. This sounds profoundly un-Nietzschean, pure Schopenhauer in fact. And Vattimo concedes as much, noting that 'on the ethical plane . . . it appears obvious that a weak ontology will have to take up the teaching of Schopenhauer'.[85]

This paradoxical argument creatively links the 'moderation' of the Superman, the idea that 'there are no facts, only interpretations; and this too is an interpretation', and the overcoming of self-interest. As argued above,[86] the moderation of the Superman lies (only) in avoiding an extreme aversive reaction to extreme nihilism—not in his accepting that the interpretation that all is interpretation is *merely* an interpretation, but rather that *even* that interpretation is an interpretation. Whereas the former reading qualifies the judgement (and thus constitutes the first step away from it) the latter reinforces it, emphasising that there is no way out of contingency (the idea embodied in the doctrine of the eternal return).

Vattimo is, however, right to acknowledge Nietzsche's alignment of interpretation and interest. Nietzsche himself is insistent on this point: 'The will to power *interprets* . . . In fact, interpretation is itself a means of becoming master of something.'[87] But it does not follow from this that acknowledging the interpretation to be an interpretation is a form of self-mastery that results in disinterested contemplation. According to Nietzsche, it is just another manifestation of the *agon* of the drives or affects: 'One may not ask: "who then interprets?" for the interpretation itself is a form of the will to power . . . not as a being, but as a process, a becoming . . . an affect'.[88] And even if it did result in disinterested contemplation, the state of disinterest itself is actually another form of interest, another way for the will to express the will to power.

In contrast, counter-interest does not take the form of disinterest, or countervailing interest. When, as for Nietzsche it always is, interpretation is interest, counter-interest is not interpretation interpreted, but rather a failure to interpret. Interpretative failure occurs when someone 'no longer has the strength to interpret', for 'exhaustion . . . changes the aspect of things, the *value of things*'. For Nietzsche, interpretation and value creation are inseparable. Whereas the strong 'involuntarily *give* to things and see them fuller, more powerful, and pregnant with future . . . the exhausted diminish and botch all they see—they impoverish the value'.[89] Examples might include those who no longer have the strength to create a fictive world, those who cannot value-posit, world-form or see-as. Nihilism is not so much caused by the failure of interpretation; it is the failure of interpretation, for ultimately interpretation and value are one and the same thing.

Vattimo, it seems, does not fully absorb Nietzsche's critique of Schopenhauer or his critique of nihilism. Arguing from the inescapability of interpretation to Schopenhauer's disinterested contemplation misses Nietzsche's point that since interpretation is interest, there can be no escape from interest either. Similarly, although Nietzsche (and Heidegger) may argue that nihilism turns back on itself in interpretation, nihilism does not turn back on itself *because* interpretation turns back on, or against itself. In Nietzsche's account, nihilism is forced to turn back on itself because interpretation (that is, value-positing) goes on forever, and nihilism can never go beyond it without also continuing to interpret.

Unlike Nietzsche and Heidegger, Vattimo does not offer a transcendental argument against nihilism, but an argument, like that of Schopenhauer on the will, based on the ultimately self-contradictory and self-cancelling nature of interpretation. Vattimo's weak ontology, or 'ontology of the weakening of Being', is not therefore in any sense equivalent to a negative ecology of Being. Not only does he fail to engage with Nietzsche's insistent materialism and biologism, and so miss the point that for Nietzsche (as, less crudely, for Heidegger) the question of nihilism is ultimately ecological, but his weak ontology unselfconsciously assumes a positive ecology of disinterested interpreters.

Sirens, Again

For interpreters, read aesthetes. Vattimo singles out the aesthetic as the model of a truly nihilistic hermeneutics in that it is 'purely contemplative and does not assume, with respect to the object, a theoretical or practical position'.[90] At the same time, he uses nihilism as the means of grounding the aesthetic, recuperating neo-Kantian aesthetic consciousness as an experience of truth precisely because 'this experience is substantially nihilistic'.[91]

Vattimo finds indications of this in Nietzsche as well, above all in the possibility, 'to which the artist bears witness', of transcending the instinct for self-preservation and achieving that 'condition of moderation that also forms the basis of the heedless disinterested hubris . . . of the *Übermensch*'.[92] On this view, the Superman is 'someone who . . . is able to look at many cultures with a gaze more aesthetic than "objective"', in effect an 'artist'.[93] Here

Vattimo echoes Schopenhauer's 'ascetic interpretation of Kantian aesthetic disinterestedness' in which aesthetic experience offered an intimation of what such disinterested contemplation might be like. Then in 'aesthetic pleasure in the beautiful . . . we are raised for the moment above all willing' and, if only for an instant, 'the storm of passions . . . and all the miseries of willing are at once calmed and appeased'.[94]

But as Nietzsche makes clear, the exhausted can botch and impoverish the experience of the aesthetic as they can anything else. The strong, whose interpretation of the world allows them to see things more fully, are exemplified by the artist who 'transforms things until they mirror his own power', for 'in art, man takes delight in himself as perfection'. But it would, Nietzsche acknowledges, be possible to imagine 'an antithetical condition, a specific anti-artisticality of instinct—a mode of being which impoverishes and attenuates things and makes them consumptive'.[95]

The anti-artist may have provided Nietzsche with his original model of weakness, not the other way around. In the essay on David Strauss, Nietzsche quotes Friedrich Vischer as saying that 'It is not always strength of will, *but weakness,* which enables *us* to transcend that longing for the beautiful experienced so profoundly "by tragic souls".' This, Nietzsche adds, is proof positive that it is weakness that frees us from the desire for beauty, a weakness that is usually recognised under another name—as 'the celebrated "healthiness" of the cultural philistines!' They 'speak of health where we see weakness, of sickness and tension where we encounter true health'.[96]

If it is weakness of will that allows the philistine to resist the beautiful, might it lead us to reconsider our understanding of Odysseus and the Sirens? In Adorno and Horkheimer's reworking of the myth, Odysseus hears the music and would have responded to its call to primordial unity had he not been constrained from doing so. He is an example of disinterest triumphing over the passions, in which the disinterested contemplation of the song is actually a form of self-interest. It is because he knows he lacks the strength of will to resist the beauty of the Sirens' song that he has himself tied to the mast. This is weakness as incontinence, but it is self-interest, not incontinence, that turns Odysseus into a philistine. The weakness of Socrates takes another form, closer to that which Aristotle calls softness. Knowing he ought to appreciate the music of the Sirens, he is nevertheless unable to do so. He does not hear the beauty of the song; he may not even hear the song as a song.

After his letter to Bacon, filled with the same despair, Chandos embarked upon a voyage. Sailing past the Sirens he heard only noises, perhaps the creaking of the oars. When he sailed back the other way, the Sirens, who had been reading Kafka, kept silent instead. He heard only noises, perhaps the creaking of the oars.

7

The Great Beast

If there be any among those common objects I doe contemne and laugh at, it is that great enemy of reason, vertue and religion, the multitude, that numerous piece of monstrosity, which taken asunder seeme men, and the reasonable creature of God, but confused together, make but one great beast, and a monstrosity more prodigious than Hydra.

Thomas Browne

Equality has had no fiercer critic than Nietzsche, whose '*fundamental* insight with respect to the genealogy of morals' is that social inequality is the source of our value concepts, and the necessary condition of value itself.[1] His rejection of equality is unequivocal. He distinguishes himself absolutely from the 'levellers' and 'preachers of equality'.[2] There is, he claims, 'no more poisonous poison': 'it seems to be preached by justice itself, while it is the *end* of justice', for 'men are not equal'.[3]

However, Nietzsche's anti-egalitarianism is not unnuanced. He does not reject equality based upon attributes that people actually share, only the imputation of equality in the face of obvious differences of strength and weakness: ' "Equality for equals, inequality for unequals"—*that* would be the true voice of justice.'[4] He therefore accepts equality up to a point; it is just that his understanding is restricted to the flat summit of 'good men' who, '*inter pares*',[5] are constrained by ties of reciprocity. But whereas 'the good are a caste, the bad [are] a mass like grains of sand'.[6] For Nietzsche, the problem with egalitarianism is not that it acknowledges equality within these two groups, but rather that it erodes the distinction between them by making equal what is unequal: 'Are we not . . . well on the way to turning mankind into *sand*? Sand! Small, soft, round, unending sand!'[7]

The metaphor proved to be a significant one for Nietzsche, because it simultaneously suggests a result, 'the desert' of nihilism,[8] and the nature of the process through which it occurs. According to Nietzsche, nihilism means that values become devalued.[9] Because value is created by valuation, and valuation, as will to power, requires social difference, the way devaluation takes place is ultimately through social change. Making empty is the result of making small. A 'law-like communism' in which each must recognize every other as equal would therefore be 'the destruction and dissolution of man, an attack on the future of man, a sign of exhaustion, a secret path towards nothingness'.[10]

The path originated, Nietzsche suggests, in the idea of equality before God. The human species endures only through sacrifice, for evolution requires that the weak perish. However, with Christianity, 'all souls became equal before God'. This was 'the most dangerous of all possible evaluations', for by designating all individuals as equal, and valuing the sick as much as, or more than, the healthy, it undermined the justification for human sacrifice, and so 'encourages a way of life that leads to the ruin of the species'.[11]

For Nietzsche, there is a clear route that leads from the New Testament's 'war against the noble and powerful'[12] to the atrocities of the French Revolution:

> The aristocratic outlook has been undermined most deeply by the lie of equality of souls; and if the belief in the 'prerogative of the majority' makes revolutions and *will continue to make them*—it is Christianity, let there be no doubt about it, *Christian* value judgement which translates every revolution into mere blood and

crime! Christianity is a revolt of everything that crawls along the ground directed against that which is *elevated*: the Gospel of the 'lowly' *makes* low.[13]

The road that leads from 'the lie of equality of souls' via the French Revolution to the 'ruin of the species' is the path of nihilism. But is it, as Nietzsche implies, also that of egalitarianism? Even on a secret path there may be detours on the way.

Permanent Revolution

What is the belief that 'makes revolutions and will continue to make them'? Is it equality, as Nietzsche claims? This, at least, was the assumption of Babeuf's Conspiracy of Equals. Even before Thermidor it had become a commonplace to say that the revolution was over. When, for example, Le Chapelier put forward his law limiting workers' associations, he argued that they had been useful while the revolution lasted, but were superfluous now the revolution was finished.[14] To such suggestions the conspirators responded that the revolution was not over as long as there were more people who could be made equal: 'one single man on earth richer, stronger than his like, than his equals, and the equilibrium is broken: crime and unhappiness are on earth'. Far from being finished, the revolution was nothing but the precursor to a still greater one.[15]

The revolution had to continue because there were more people to be included among the equals and, if necessary, it would continue even at the expense of that level of culture or equality that already existed. Maréchal may have gone beyond some of his comrades in proclaiming 'Let the arts perish, if need be, as long as real equality remains',[16] but Babeuf too was clearly a leveller. He suspected that the counter-revolutionaries in the Vendée had been decimated by Jacobin forces in order to facilitate the distribution of resources among a smaller population, and argued that true egalitarianism required not a reduced population in order sustain a higher level equality among those that remained, but rather shared deprivation for all.[17]

Babeuf's argument here is precisely that which Nietzsche attributes to egalitarians: equality precludes the possibility of sacrificing some people for the benefit of others. Yet the target of Babeuf's remarks is not the ancien regime, but rather the egalitarianism of the Jacobins themselves. The point of equality, he suggests, is not making some limited number of people more equal, even if they constitute a majority, but rather making as many people as possible equal, even if that means equality at a lower level. The revolution must continue not so much because equality is imperfect, but because its scope has been too limited.

Reflecting on Babeuf's ill-fated project, Proudhon recognised the issue it was trying to address, but he did not see Babeuf's programme as the solution, complaining that it 'reduced all citizens to the lowest level'.[18] And as such, Proudhon argued, it was inegalitarian rather than egalitarian—though in the opposite sense to that in which the term is usually understood, for whereas 'property is the exploitation of the weak by the strong; community is the exploitation of the strong by the weak'.[19] Marx also criticised the primitive communism of Babeuf as motivated merely by the desire to level down,[20] but nevertheless identified strongly with the idea that revolution must continue, not perhaps, as Maréchal had argued, for as long as there was one man raised above his equals, but at least as long as one class was raised above the rest. As he famously remarked after 1848: 'it is our interest and our task to make the revolution permanent, until all more or less possessing classes have been forced out of their position of dominance, [and] the proletariat has conquered state power'.[21]

Marx's simultaneous rejection of Babeuf's communism and acceptance of his motivation for continuing the revolution requires explanation. The ultimate basis of this move may perhaps be found in Pufendorf's threefold distinction between private property, positive community, and negative community.[22] This meant that there were potentially three ways for equality to be realised. If property is private, individuals will have whatever they have in equal shares to the exclusion of every other proprietor. In positive community, where property is in common ownership, each individual will have exactly the same as all other proprietors, to the exclusion of nonproprietors, while in negative community each individual, without exclusion or exception, will have equal access to property but no property rights, either individual or collective, because property, as such, will not exist.

As Pufendorf pointed out, the key difference is the question of exclusivity:

> Both positive community as well as proprietorship imply an exclusion of others from the thing which is said to be common or proper . . . Therefore, just as things could not be said to be proper to a man, if he were the only being in the world, so the things from the use of which no man is excluded, or which, in other words, belong to no man more than to another, should be called common in the former [negative] and not in the latter [positive] meaning of the term.[23]

The unfolding narrative of revolution reflects these distinctions. To the Jacobin acceptance of private property, Babeuf has juxtaposed a form of positive community. Both Proudhon and Marx explicitly criticised him on this basis,[24] but whereas Proudhon favoured a synthesis of positive community and private property, Marx seems to have looked beyond positive community to a form of communism that was still more inclusive and utopian, a form of negative community governed by the principle 'from each according to his abilities, to each according to his needs'.[25]

However, Marx postpones the realisation of this community to the post-revolutionary transition from socialism to communism and offers a conception of permanent revolution that itself potentially contains two limits, the proletariat and the state. The discrepancy did not go unnoticed. If the revolution was over when the proletariat controlled the state, what of those outside the proletariat and beyond the boundaries of the state? As Bakunin noted, Marx conspicuously excluded from the agents of revolution the *Lumpenproletariat*, 'that great mass, those millions of the uncultivated, the disinherited, the miserable, the illiterates . . . that great *rabble of the people*', and by affirming the role of the state reinscribed the chief limitation of the Jacobin republic itself, which 'hardly knew man and recognized the citizen only'.[26] In contrast, Bakunin advocated 'the emancipation and widest possible expansion of social life', by which he meant 'the natural mode of existence of the human collectivity, independent of any contract.' Society therefore included not only those inhabitants of a state excluded from full citizenship, but also the rest of humankind, beyond the borders of the nation state.[27] One of Bakunin's followers drew the obvious conclusion: 'The revolution cannot be confined to a single country: it is obliged under pain of annihilation to spread.'[28]

Trotsky's reformulation of the idea of permanent revolution picks up both of Bakunin's objections. Believing that 'The proletariat, in order to consolidate its power, cannot but widen the base of the revolution',[29] he argues that 'permanent revolution . . . means a revolution which makes no compromise with any single form of class rule . . . a revolution whose every successive stage is rooted in the preceding one and which can end only in the complete liquidation of class society'; and just as there can be no class limit, so there can be no national boundary: 'the socialist revolution begins on national foundations—but it cannot be completed within these foundations'. Every limit must be sloughed off by society; 'revolutions . . . do not allow society to achieve equilibrium'; rather, 'society keeps on changing its skin'.[30]

Although one is concerned with economic and the other with political goods, there is a parallel between the argument made for an ongoing revolution in order to end exclusion from property and the argument made for a form of permanent revolution that will prevent exclusion from revolution itself. In both cases, there is a potential limit—represented by positive community and socialism in one country—which is exceeded not on the basis that those outside the limit are necessarily the equals of those within, but rather that the existence of the limit perpetuates a form of inequality which otherwise might not exist. Rather than making access dependent on a certain level of productivity or a certain level of development, negative community and permanent revolution offer to the unequal (unproductive individuals, undeveloped classes and peoples alike) access to that on which they might otherwise have no claim.

The parallel serves to highlight the changing relationship between inclusivity and equality in the earlier example. In the Conspiracy of Equals, equality demanded a greater inclusivity, which potentially resulted in the loss of social goods or diminished access to finite resources. Marx's alternative to the levelling down involved in positive community goes a stage further. Negative community may level out so completely that it dissolves everything it touches. For this reason, as Pufendorf notes, critics argued that it was 'opposed to human, that is, rational nature, appropriate only to animals, and unsocial'.[31] If everyone can just take what they need, the ideal of egalitarian inclusiveness is extended to the point where it dissolves the concept of property, and with it the possibility of equality, or any form of distributive justice. Eventually, of course, negative community undermines species being itself.

Making Equal

Nietzsche, too, was concerned with the relationship between equality and inclusivity. In his view, equalisation involves the inclusion of something unequal into the community of the equal. Assuming that there is no such thing as irrelevant difference he argues that the process of equalisation is always accompanied by loss. The pattern can be found in a variety of contexts. The basis of language and logic is, Nietzsche suggests, 'to treat as equal what is merely similar': concepts arise 'from the equation of unequal things', and 'words make the uncommon common'. This is, he claims, the Procrustean nature of all cognitive functioning.[32]

However, because equalisation involves subsuming 'a sense impression into an existing series',[33] it is less a matter of fitting something to a pre-existing pattern than of assimilating it into a living organism:

> All thought, judgement, perception, considered as comparison, has as its precondition a *'positing* of equality', and earlier still a *'making* equal'. The process of making equal is the same as the process of incorporation of appropriated material in the amoeba.[34]

There is therefore a direct analogy between the formation of thought and the formation of society, for both are the product of equalisation in the face of infinite difference. Even the formation of logic has 'the herd instinct in the background'.[35]

The point at which the cognitive and the social converge is the law. Nietzsche posits equality as the basis of all contracts and law on the grounds that justice depends on the parties' involved being of equal power.[36] Contracts, he suggests, continue to exist only for as long as the parties to them remain equal; 'an end is put to them if one party has *become* decisively *weaker* than the other'.[37] What then is the fate of the law when, perhaps due to the consequences of decadence, those over whom jurisdiction is exercised are unequal to the law?

The question preoccupies Nietzsche, and he considers it in terms both of the relationship of the criminal to society, and of parasite to host. On the one hand, he suggests that in order to maintain an equilibrium 'a community in which all regard themselves as equivalent' may treat a transgressor 'as one who is not

equivalent, as one of the weak standing outside it'.[38] Being outside
society means being left in the state of nature, which may well lead
to extermination. But this is in a sense only what justice demands,
for all individuals represent either ascending or descending trajectories, and while the former must be preserved at all costs, the
latter 'can be accorded little value, and elementary fairness
demands that he *take away* as little as possible from the well-
constituted. He is no better than a parasite to them.' As a parasite
on society, it is sometimes 'indecent to go on living'.[39]

Conversely, the criminal/parasite may be tolerated. Nietzsche
gives diverging interpretations of this process.[40] One way in
which this might occur is if the power and self-confidence of a
community grew to such an extent that it would allow those who
harm it to go unpunished: ' "Of what concern are these parasites
to me?" it would be entitled to say. "May they live and prosper:
I am strong enough to allow that!" ' In this case, the result would
be the 'self-cancellation of justice' at the discretion of the
strong.[41] Eventually, however, there might come 'a point in the
history of society when it becomes so pathologically soft and
tender that among other things it sides even with those who
harm it, criminals'.[42] In this case, society becomes so weak that
it does not even try to punish or exclude those who will undermine it. It is 'a society that no longer has the strength to excrete'.[43]
With this move, the herd morality of compassion draws its ultimate self-defeating conclusion.

How are these possibilities related? In the first case, Nietzsche
describes a form of equality that demands the exclusion of the
unequal; in the second, a form of benign indifference that tolerates
the unequal outside the equalising protection of the law; in the
third, an inclusivity that undermines the law. Nietzsche speculated
that equalisation might have developed because it offered some
competitive advantage, but that it was 'held in check by considerations of success'. In the last example 'the fundamental inclination
to posit as equal' is *not* 'held in check'. Instead of being so strong

that it is able to sustain parasites with indifference, society allows itself to become infested with them.

Nietzsche does not fully align this account of 'making equal' conceived as assimilation with that of 'making low' in which equalisation is described in terms of levelling. They are clearly compatible insofar as the absorption of higher types by the herd involves a levelling down, but the model of assimilation is also open to another outcome: the absorption of the less than equal. The former exemplifies the herd morality at work, the latter the self-negation of the herd morality. Could they nevertheless be part of a single process?

Repugnant Conclusions

The genealogy of permanent revolution given above provides some clues as to how such a process might be articulated. First, there is levelling down within a given population of the kind advocated by the Conspiracy of Equals. Then there is Babeuf's point that a larger population at a lower level of well-being is preferable to a smaller one at a higher level. This is something other than simple egalitarianism, for if both populations were made up of equals, there would be nothing to choose between them. And finally there is Marx's rejection of egalitarianism in favour of a version of negative community in which resources are available to all in proportion to need.

These are distinct arguments that give rise to distinct objections. The first is simply egalitarianism, open to the criticism that if equality makes nobody any better off it is effectively pointless (indeed, that it becomes impossible to specify the sense in which equality really is better). The second assumes equality but also makes an implicit appeal to total utility, or at least to the happiness of the greater number. The potential objection to this type of argument is the implication that having an enormous number of people living lives barely worth living would be better than even a very large population with a very high quality of life, a possibility Parfit has called the Repugnant Conclusion. Finally, there are objections to negative community (which does not presuppose equality at all). These usually take a Malthusian form. If there are no boundaries and uncontrolled access to finite goods, then a society is vulnerable to the tragedy of the commons, in which the resource in question diminishes and eventually disappears due to the absence of any restrictions on its use.[44]

Because they are philosophically distinct these arguments are rarely considered together. However, juxtaposing them may reveal something that is obscured when taken separately, namely the extent to which one might lead to the next. Parfit's Mere Addition Paradox (not necessarily a paradox for total utilitarians) suggests one way in which this might happen. In its simplest form it starts with a population of equals at a high level, adds some extra people at a lower level outside the existing population (say the inhabitants of a previously undiscovered continent or planet), equalises the two groups separately (not necessarily levelling them down), and then unites them to form a single larger population at a lower level than the first equal population. If you are comfortable with each of these steps, and repeat them, you eventually end up with the Repugnant Conclusion. You would in effect have created a Utility Monster (a term Parfit borrows from Nozick) capable of devouring all the goods in the world in order to distribute them ever more thinly among an ever larger number—an outcome distinct from but similar in effect to a tragedy of the commons (which assumes scarcity but not equality).[45]

Nietzsche's account of the criminal/parasite contains the same elements. It begins with a finite group of equals contracted within the law and potentially ends with a society from which no one can be excluded. Along the way there are first equals within the law, then equals within the law and the criminal/weak outside, and then the criminal and weak are reincluded. Unlike Parfit, Nietzsche offers an explanation of where his extra people come from. A descending trajectory produces relative failure, weakness as opposed to strength. Where there is equality, it generates inequality. Where there is law it makes unequal to the law. If the weak are excluded from the law, they become criminals standing outside the law alongside those who were too weak to be included in the first place, and if they are reincluded then existing law has to be remade and contracts made between all who are equals at this lower level. This will include both those who were party to the previous contract (if they have been levelled down) and those who were unequal to the previous law and so excluded from it.

The process is never described in full, but similar cases in which failure extends equality, and equality consolidates failure, are easy to imagine. For example, suppose there is a club for people who can run a four-minute mile; through age or illness, some become weaker and slower than they used to be and are automatically excluded from membership; rather than allow them to be permanently excluded, the club committee relaxes the rules: now the club is open to those with a time of less than four minutes and fifteen seconds; the excluded members return along with a host of less athletic newcomers; in time, they too begin to slow down, and the process is repeated. If, as Nietzsche claims, 'tiredness is the shortest path to *equality*',[46] and equality is the secret path to nothingness, tiredness may be a shortcut to nothingness as well.

It is important to note, however, that we cannot arrive at this destination just by levelling down. In levelling down, just as much as with equality *inter pares*, there is a limit below which no one may fall, namely that of the worst off in the initial population. The Repugnant Conclusion can only be reached if the level to which a population has been levelled down is transformed into the level from which it levels out. Only in levelling out, where extra people are added at every step, is there no limit to how low you can go. But in order to level out, there has to be some acceptance of extra people at a lower level. This is not itself egalitarian. If simple failure creates extra people, in the real world (as opposed to thought experiments) it requires the counter-interest of the relatively strong to sustain them: Christian compassion (as Nietzsche suggests), total utilitarianism, tolerance, or (as Nietzsche elsewhere suggests) sheer indifference, might all potentially have the same effect.

The cumulative dynamic is therefore not so much egalitarian as extraegalitarian in that it explicitly favours a move from egalitarian to inegalitarian distributions. It both exceeds and stands outside egalitarianism, while always presupposing and returning to it. What would such an extraegalitarianism involve? One way to describe it would be as the conjunction of two principles: (i) individuals or groups within a collectivity should be as equal as possible, even if no one is any better off as a result; (ii) there's nothing wrong with extra people, even if they are not equal to those there already. The first is an egalitarian principle open to a levelling down objection: how is it better for people to be equal even if no one is any better off? The second, in its most obvious philosophical form, is a total utilitarian one open to an egalitarian objection: why create inequality where none existed before? All extraegalitarianism does is use one to justify the other: levelling down is justified by increased numbers; increased numbers by further equality. Levelling out furthers both equality and utility, but not at the same time.

Given that the Repugnant Conclusion might be defended on some conjunction of egalitarianism and utilitarianism, what is repugnant about it? The most widely cited objection to both levelling down and levelling out is that they undermine value: levelling down removes the inequalities necessary in order to generate particular things of value, while levelling out progressively removes all possibility of higher forms of value from the world. Maréchal's 'Let the arts perish . . .' acknowledges and accepts the consequences of the former argument, but most commentators have followed Nietzsche in considering it unacceptable. Even an egalitarian like Thomas Nagel admits to striking 'a mildly Nietzschean note' when he argues that 'a society which supports creative achievement and encourages maximum levels of excellence will have to accept and exploit stratification and hierarchy', and that 'no egalitarianism can be right which would permit haute cuisine, haute couture, and exquisite houses to disappear'.[47]

Similarly, Parfit, though rejecting the Nietzschean view that it would justify great suffering, nevertheless argues that 'even if some change brings a great net benefit to those who are affected, it is a change for the worse if it involves the loss of one of the best things in life'.[48] He therefore imagines the Mere Addition Paradox as a series of steps in which the best things in life disappear one by one. In common with most modern philosophers, he supposes the best things in life to be aesthetic. So at the first, Mozart's music is lost, then Haydn's; then Venice is destroyed, then Verona, until eventually all that is left is a life of Muzak and potatoes. The sequence may be personal, but the nature of the examples is meant to be uncontroversial. Along the way, any of these irreplaceable things might be taken as the unacceptable loss, the limit beyond which no more extra people could be added.

Alternatively, each step could be taken as a means of disposing of these valueless luxuries once and for all, a programme for a philistine demography, a negative ecology of value. As Nagel observes, 'it is not always easy to prevent egalitarianism . . . from infecting other values',[49] and it is for this reason Nietzsche correctly identifies it as nihilism's secret ally. But as Nietzsche also points out, there is nothing nihilistic about equality itself; it is only nihilistic if the less than equal are introduced into the equation and everyone is levelled out as a consequence. Equality is the means, not the end, and nihilism eventually exceeds equality. Revolutionary egalitarianism is indeed extraegalitarian in just this sense, in that the argument for continuing revolution is based upon the idea that there are extra people who could and should be included even if the population is perfectly equal already.

What makes all this nihilistic is not just the loss of value (either in the form of particular goods or of average utility) but the potential disappearance of what at the start of the process is the good being distributed—notably property, citizenship, equality itself. Interpreted this way, extraegalitarianism represents not a utopian distribution, but a form of socially realised scepticism about value. Equality already functions like this in the case of positional goods where sharing in and diminishing the value of are effected simultaneously. Extraegalitarianism takes this further: it implicitly registers the ambiguity of all goods. The only uncertainty is: 'How far can it go?'

The Great Beast

Simone Weil puts the question another way: 'Would a society in which only gravity reigned be able to exist?' Phrased like this, the question might as well be Nietzsche's.[50] Zarathustra's nemesis is the dwarf, the 'Spirit of Gravity', that draws him toward the abyss. And not just Zarathustra. Since Copernicus, man has been on a steep slope rolling 'towards nothingness'.[51]

Weil interprets her own question much as Nietzsche might have done. Society is composed of a balance of ascending and descending forces.[52] It maintains its equilibrium and keeps away evil 'by forming as it were a barrier'. Injustice involves disregarding this limit, and so 'the successive and compensating ruptures of equilibrium constitute the image of a succession of injustices and expiations'.[53] However, a 'society of criminals' would destroy this barrier,[54] for there would be no ascent to balance the descent, and no expiation for injustice. Society as a whole would then no longer have any way of maintaining its equilibrium and would succumb to the entropy of evil. A society in which gravity reigns would be 'a descent into the without-limit'.[55]

The ethical content of Weil's gravity is the precise inverse of Nietzsche's—hers is characterised by egotism, his by selflessness—and yet it works the same way. In both cases, it is an ineluctable heaviness that encompasses the failure of individuals to distinguish themselves from society, and the failure of society to close itself to harmful or lesser individuals. Both Weil and Nietzsche use a mix of scientific and sociological imagery to conjoin a vertical axis (gravity, falling) with a horizontal one (equilibrium, absorption) and to suggest that extending the social base to allow for uncompensated descent will inevitably lower the overall level.

Weil calls the society in which gravity reigns the 'Great Beast'. Inflected though it is by Christian apocalyptic, her primary point of reference is Plato, who in the *Republic* derides the Sophists for merely echoing the opinions of the multitude:

> It is as if a man were acquiring the knowledge of the humours and desires of a great strong beast he had in his keeping, how it is to be approached and touched, and when and by what things it is made most savage or gentle, yes, and the several sounds it is wont to utter on the occasion of each, and again what sounds uttered by another make it tame or fierce, and after mastering this knowledge by living with the creature and by lapse of time call it wisdom, and should construct thereof a system.[56]

There is, Plato argues, no difference between this and the man who takes on board the political and aesthetic judgements of the crowd, and is then compelled 'to give the public what it likes'.

However, Weil's beast is now adapted to the division of labour: 'since the beast is huge and men are tiny, each one is differently placed in relation to it . . . we may imagine that among those with the task of grooming it, one takes charge of a knee, another of a claw, another of the neck, another of the back'.[57] They all take their own activity as normative and each develops a professional morality in accordance with it. This allows men to commit acts of greater virtue or vice than they might otherwise do, and also opens the way for the 'society of criminals' whose professional morality is itself vice. As Durkheim eventually realised, the division of labour has no limits, so even 'the criminal no longer appears as an utterly unsociable creature, a sort of parasitic element, a foreign unassailable body, introduced into the bosom of society. He plays a normal role in society.'[58]

Nietzsche, too, had something like this imagery in mind, though he perceived the social mechanism less clearly. In *Daybreak* he refers to the promised socialist utopia as the time when 'the day of the *bestia triumphans* dawns in all its glory'.[59] But it was his early admirer Gabriele D'Annunzio who made explicit the identification of this beast with that of Plato. In his essay 'La bestia elettiva' (1892), he rehearses Nietzsche's arguments against equality, and in *Le vergini delle rocce* (the novel in which material from the essay is recycled) he refers to parliamentarians as 'stableboys of *la gran bestia*', like the man in Plato's parable.[60]

Following Nietzsche, D'Annunzio complains that 'While Nature tends to multiply all differences without limit, Democracy tends instead to render all men equal.' He too looks for 'a new oligarchy' that will harness 'the masses for its own benefit . . . destroying all empty dreams of equality and justice'. Then the consequences of egalitarianism will be reversed. Humanity will be divided into a superior race, 'lifted up by the sheer energy of its will', to whom all shall be permitted, and an inferior, who will be allowed 'little or close to nothing'. Ruthless selectivity and exclusivity can once again come into play. Prolonging the lives of the sick would be like 'passing over the most vigorous trees in a wood so as to nurse some . . . common weed'. D'Annunzio concludes with Nietzsche's own tragedy of the commons: 'Life is a fountain of delight but where the rabble also drinks the wells are poisoned.'[61]

The great democratic beast to which D'Annunzio alludes threatens to appear in many guises—as a forest of weeds, a poisoned well, a desert of sand. But it is always that form of society where boundaries are so permeable that its values are compromised by the inclusion of those who will undermine it. If subsequently levelled down, it makes little difference whether society is conceived as expanding laterally through the division of labour, or vertically through the enfranchisement of the masses. In both cases, the eventual result is a levelling out which ensures that the new aggregation will form less than its constituent parts.

As Thomas Browne recognised, something of this is already implicit in Plato's parable. He illustrated the phenomenon of collective diminution by using the example of an abacus, where a bead on one row is worth a fifth of that on the next: when they form part of the great beast 'three or foure men together come short in account of one man placed by himself below them [where one is worth five of those above]'.[62]

However, when the great beast reappears in the twentieth century, it has undergone a subtle metamorphosis. Plato's beast shows how society can bring down to its own level those who should know better—the educated to the level of the ignorant and the gentleman to the commoner—but this is not a metaphor for the limitless degeneration of society itself. With the coming of modernity there is a shift, as the great beast becomes that which is levelled out. Now, it no longer has a limit. It has become a form of socially constructed nihilism, a way humans join together to become less than they might otherwise be.

Passive Revolution

For Vincenzo Cuoco, the Neapolitan political writer who was himself a protagonist in the short-lived Parthenopean Republic of 1799, Plato's great beast may have offered an alternative model for revolution. Although the author of a philosophical novel titled *Platone in Italia,* Cuoco rejected ideal republics as too utopian, instead arguing that any successful revolution must gratify the wishes of the people: 'This is the entire secret of revolutions: know what it is that all the people want, and do it.'[63]

However, although Cuoco saw no other way of activating a revolution than that of inducting the people, he acknowledged that there were two ways this could come about: if the revolution is active the people unite themselves with the revolutionaries; if it is passive, 'the revolutionaries unite themselves with the people'.[64] Of the two, Cuoco considered active revolutions the more effective because the people act of their own accord and in their own interest, whereas in a passive revolution 'the agent of government, divines the spirit of the people and presents to them what they desire'.[65] In response to the objection that it is impossible to know what the people want, because a 'people' does not speak, he advocates precisely the technique that Plato mocked the Sophists for following when they made a system of the sounds uttered by the great beast—noting and interpreting other less articulate expressions of the popular will and then acting accordingly. Although a people stays silent, 'everything speaks for it: its ideas speak for it, its prejudices, its customs, its needs'.[66]

Taking on the opinions of the people is the way to expand the base of the revolution. Indeed, the two operations are potentially identical. The only way to co-opt the people is to allow yourself to be co-opted by them, even when, as Cuoco makes clear was the case in Naples, the people are the 'lazy *lazzaroni*', Marx's *Lumpenproletariat*.[67] The Neapolitan revolution did not fail because it was a passive revolution, rather, it was a failed passive revolution, where the interests of the revolutionaries and the people were irreconcilable. Gramsci claimed that Cuoco's use of 'passive revolution' was no more than a cue for his own.[68] But read as a version of the great beast, the continuities between Cuoco and Gramsci emerge more clearly, and with them the possibility that passive revolution might be more than a type of failed revolution or prototype of counterrevolution.

In order to explore this possibility, it is necessary to return to the beginning of the narrative, the point at which the history of revolution first appeared to have come to an end. Gramsci maintained that the French Revolution 'found its widest class limits' in the Jacobins' maintenance of the Le Chapelier law. It was for this reason that the Jacobins 'always remained on bourgeois ground'. 'Permanent revolution', which the Jacobins appeared to be initiating, had reached its limit. Paradoxically, however, Gramsci argues that 'the formula of Permanent Revolution put into practice in the active phase of the French Revolution' later 'found its "completion" in the parliamentary regime', which 'realised the permanent hegemony of the urban class over the entire population'. This was achieved through a combination of force and consent, widening the economic base, and absorbing successful members of the lower classes into the bourgeoisie. In this manner, 'The "limit" which the Jacobins had come up against in the Le Chapelier law . . . was transcended and pushed progressively back.'[69]

According to Gramsci, something similar occurred in the Risorgimento, which was also characterised after 1848 by the formation of an ever more extensive ruling class. In this case, too, 'the formation of this class involved the gradual but continuous absorption . . . of the active elements produced by allied groups—and even those which came from antagonistic groups and seemed irreconcilably hostile'. The result could be described as ' "revolution" without a "revolution" or as "passive revolution"'.[70] For in a passive revolution 'The thesis alone in fact develops to the full its potential for struggle, up to the point where it absorbs even the so-called representatives of the antithesis: it is precisely in this that the passive revolution or revolution/restoration consists.'[71]

Juxtaposed like this, Gramsci's arguments carry the clear implication that permanent revolution is, or can only be completed as, 'passive revolution'. It is an inference that he never explicitly makes, and it is one his commentators decline to draw as well, yet it is suggested not just by historical analyses, but by his own fragmentary attempts to reconcile his conceptual frameworks. His basic conceptual opposition is between the war of movement and the war of position, and he identifies the former with the concept of permanent revolution, the latter with the concept of hegemony.[72] However, where hegemony is rule by 'permanently organised consent',[73] like that realised by the urban class over the entire French population under the parliamentary regime, it may function as the completion of permanent revolution represented by the Jacobin experience from 1789 to Thermidor. Hence, it is consistent for Gramsci to claim that 'the 48ist formula of "Permanent Revolution" is expanded and transcended in political science by the formula of "civil hegemony"'.[74]

But Gramsci not only identifies the war of position with civil hegemony, he also identifies it with passive revolution. He asks himself whether Cuoco's concept of 'passive revolution' can be related to the concept of 'war of position' in contrast to 'war of manoeuvre', and whether there may be historical periods in which there exists 'an absolute identity' between them in which 'the two concepts must be considered identical'.[75] Gramsci clearly thinks so and identifies Europe post-1848 and 1871 as examples. So if the war of manoeuvre gives way to the war of position, in which permanent revolution is transcended by civil hegemony, does this not also imply that permanent revolution is transcended by passive revolution?

Gramsci avoids this implication for a reason, namely that he wants to save the concept of passive revolution for specifically counter-revolutionary attempts to co-opt the forces of revolution to its own ends—the restoration, the state-led passive revolution of the Risorgimento, and fascism itself. But in fact there is no reason why the concept of passive revolution cannot be considered as politically neutral as that of the war of position, or of hegemony itself. And this becomes clear in the threefold distinction Gramsci makes between (i) the ancien regime, whose ruling classes 'did not construct an organic passage from other classes into their own, that is, to enlarge their class sphere'; (ii) the bourgeoisie, which 'poses itself as an organism in continuous movement, capable of absorbing the entire society, assimilating it to its own cultural and economic level' but which has become 'saturated'; and (iii) a class really able to assimilate the whole of society that would bring about 'the end of the State and of law—rendered useless since they will have exhausted their function and will have been absorbed by civil society'.[76] Both the latter two are classic passive revolutions, absorbing their antitheses. The difference between them is that the former, bourgeois revolution is a raising up which of its very nature must reach a limit or point of saturation, whereas the proletarian version of passive revolution, which culminates in the end of the state, has no lower limit.

If these passive revolutions are differentiated only by being limited or limitless, then this carries the implication that if any passive revolution were to continue indefinitely, it would inevitably become permanent revolution. A class that absorbs its antithesis (passive revolution) will, unless it reaches saturation, become the class that absorbs the whole of society. (As the state is of its very nature a class state, the class that absorbs the whole of society will also reabsorb the state into civil society.) According to Gramsci, the state in the West is 'only an outer ditch', behind which lie the robust institutions of civil society.[77] That outer ditch marks the class limit that restricts the scope of passive revolution; as the state is reabsorbed, the ditch becomes an open border, and Gramsci's account of permanent revolution regains its nihilistic edge.

On the Edge

Do these fragments from the history of revolution provide glimpses of Nietzsche's secret path? Nietzsche's critique of egalitarianism highlights both its nihilistic potential and the role of inclusivity in realising that potential. He identifies egalitarianism with nihilism on the basis that if value presupposes inequality, equality must undermine value. But his argument suggests that even if equality is a form of nihilism, nihilism is not necessarily always egalitarian. To the question what is egalitarianism and where are its limits? Nietzsche answers that there are two types: the egalitarianism of mutual recognition between equals, and the egalitarianism of levelling down. Both have an internal limit, but in the latter case the limit may be used to pivot from levelling down to levelling out, opening up equality to those below the existing threshold. Egalitarianism in this sense is incompatible with equality as a state, in that it is constantly prompting revaluation in favour of the less than equal, and returning to equality only via inequality.

Each of the fragments above describes a moment of disequilibrium when the argument pivots from levelling down to levelling out. Such moments appear both within the revolutionary tradition itself—in the moves from equal property to negative community, from revolution to permanent revolution—and in the counter-revolutionary response of Nietzsche, D'Annunzio and others. Less obviously, they are reflected in the transformations of the great beast. In Plato, the great beast is merely a case of levelling down. Reconceptualised by Simone Weil, the great beast becomes the society where gravity reigns, a society where there is no longer any limit to entropy. Something similar happens with the idea of passive revolution; Cuoco picks up the idea of an inarticulate people absorbing the elite, and turns it into the idea of passive revolution in which the revolutionary elite absorb the people, taking on their opinions in process. In Gramsci's hands, this process of extending the class base of revolution is implicitly identified with permanent revolution, a revolution that ends by dissolving the state and with it the possibility of revolution itself.

Negative community, the great beast, passive revolution—all are potentially a means of arriving at and extending the desert of nihilism, their very limitlessness the model of permanent revolution spreading out across the empty space of the universe. Seen from this perspective, the world has never seemed so open. We do not even need to borrow Nietzsche's sponge to wipe away the horizon. Negation, it seems, is not so much the erasure of the line as an inability to hold the line. Pivoting out rather than turning back, we realise too late: the line was just an edge to fall from.

Abbreviations

Unless otherwise indicated, Nietzsche's works are referred to by section numbers.

A   *The Antichrist*
BGE   *Beyond Good and Evil*
BT   *The Birth of Tragedy*
D   *Daybreak*
EH   *Ecce Homo*
GM   *On the Genealogy of Morals*
GS   *The Gay Science*
HH   *Human, All Too Human* (2 vols.)
KGW   *Kritische Gesamtausgabe: Werke*
TI   *Twilight of the Idols*
UM   *Untimely Meditations*
WP   *The Will to Power*
WS   *The Wanderer and his Shadow*
Z   *Thus Spoke Zarathustra*

Notes

Philistinism

1. T. W. Adorno, *Aesthetic Theory*, tr. C. Lenhardt, London, 1984, p. 342, p. 454.

2. D. J. Taylor, 'In a philistine age, who is still willing to speak up for Auntie?', *Independent on Sunday*, 25 July, 2010 ; S. Byrnes, 'A government of Philistines' www.newstatesman.com, 24 July, 2010.

3. F. Furedi, *Where Have All the Intellectuals Gone?: Confronting 21st Century Philistinism*, London, 2004.

4. *Independent on Sunday*, 12 November 1995, p. 8.

5. T. Ali, 'The BBC Goes Tabloid', *Literary Review*, December 1995, p. 17.

6. G. Walden, 'Patronage is All', ibid., p. 11.

7. J. Budden, letter, *Opera*, no. 43, 1992, p. 893.

8. R. Crichton, letter, ibid., p. 1152.

9. T. Eagleton, *Times Literary Supplement*, 24 November 1995, p. 6.

10. Adorno, *Aesthetic Theory*, p. 454.

11. M. Thompson, *Rubbish Theory*, Oxford, 1972, pp. 103–30.

12. H. Richter, *Dada: Art and Anti-Art*, London, 1965, p. 90.

13. Ibid., p. 89.

14. See for example, D. Cooper, ed., *A Companion to Aesthetics*, Oxford 1992, and M. Kelly ed., *Encyclopedia of Aesthetics*, 4 vols, Oxford, 1998.

15 Although see R. Taylor, *Art, an Enemy of the People*, Atlantic Highlands, NJ, 1978; J. Gimpel, *Against Art and Artists*, Edinburgh, 1991; A. Gell, 'The Technology of Enchantment and the Enchantment of Technology', in J. Coote and A. Shelton, eds., *Anthropology, Art and Aesthetics*, Oxford, 1992, pp. 40–63; M. Bull, 'Philistinism and Fetishism', *Art History*, vol. 17, 1994, pp. 127–31; S. Home, *Art Strike Handbook*, London, 1989, and J. Roberts and D. Beech, *The Philistine Controversy*, London, 2002.

16 B. Herrnstein Smith, *Contingencies of Value: Alternative Perspectives for Critical Theory*, Cambridge, MA, 1988, p. 137.

17 S. Connor, *Theory and Cultural Value*, Oxford, 1992, p. 59.

18 Ibid., p. 98.

19 M. Hunter and D. Wootton, 'New Histories of Atheism', in M. Hunter and D. Wootton, eds., *Atheism from the Reformation to the Enlightenment*, Oxford, 1992, p. 25.

20 A. C. Kors, *Atheism in France, 1650–1729*, Princeton, 1990, vol. 1, p. 17.

21 Quoted in N. Davidson, 'Unbelief and Atheism in Italy, 1500–1700', in Hunter and Wootton, *Atheism*, p. 56.

22 M. Hunter, 'The Problem of "Atheism" in Early Modern England', *Transactions of the Royal Historical Society*, 5th series, no. 35, 1985, p. 138.

23 F. Bacon, *Essays*, London, 1975, p. 50.

24 Quoted in Kors, *Atheism in France*, p. 28.

25 P. Bayle, *Pensées diverses sur la comète*, Paris, 1939, vol. 2, p. 5 ff.

26 D. Hume, *Enquiry Concerning Human Understanding*, Oxford, 1975, p 149.

27 See, for example, Kors, *Atheism in France*, p. 27.

28 But see T. Gregory, *Theophrastus Redivivus: Erudizione e ateismo nel Seicento*, Naples, 1979.

29 Bacon, *Essays*, p. 50.

30 R. Cudworth, *The True Intellectual System of the Universe*, London 1845, vol. 1, p. 540.

31 See R. Tuck, 'The "Christian Atheism" of Thomas Hobbes', in Hunter and Wootton, *Atheism*, pp. 111–30.

32   T. Hobbes, *Leviathan*, Cambridge, 1991, pp. 88–90.

33   D. Berman, *A History of Atheism in Britain*, London, 1988, p. 61.

34   See P. Marshall, *Demanding the Impossible: A History of Anarchism*, London, 1992.

35   J. Bentham, *Works*, London, 1843, vol. 2, p. 498.

36   Quoted in Marshall, *Demanding the Impossible*, p. 432.

37   Ibid., p. 488.

38   W. Godwin, *Enquiry Concerning Political Justice*, Oxford, 1971, p. 18.

39   Ibid., p. 102.

40   See M.A. Gillespie, *Nihilism before Nietzsche*, Chicago, 1995, pp. 275–6, n. 5.

41   J. Radowitz, quoted in J. Goudsblom, *Nihilism and Culture*, Oxford, 1980, p. 5.

42   S. Kravchinsky, quoted in Gillespie, *Nihilism before Nietzsche*, p. 140.

43   D. Pisarev, quoted in C. Moser, *Anti-Nihilism in the Russian Novel of the 1860s*, The Hague, 1964, p. 24.

44   Quoted in ibid., p. 163

45   Quoted in ibid., p. 111.

46   F. Nietzsche, *The Birth of Tragedy*, tr. W. Kaufmann (hereafter BT), New York, 1967, 5.

47   Nietzsche, *Ecce Homo*, tr. R. J. Hollingdale (hereafter EH), Harmondsworth, 1979, p. 79.

48   Quoted in Goudsblom, *Nihilism and Culture*, p. 5.

49   J. and W. Grimm, *Deutsches Wörterbuch*, Leipzig 1889, vol. 7, pp. 1826–7.

50   G. Eismann, *Robert Schumann*, Leipzig 1956, vol. 1, p. 87. See also D. Arendt, 'Das Philistertum des 19. Jahrhunderts', *Der Monat*, no. 21, May 1969, pp. 33–49.

51   So, for example, Edward Feser attacks the "new atheism" as a form of philistinism, see "The New Philistinism", *The American*, 26 March, 2010.

52   M. Arnold, *Culture and Anarchy*, New Haven, 1994, p. 73.

53   Ibid., p. 70.

54 Ibid., p. 71.
55 Ibid., p. 68.
56 Ibid., p. 35.
57 Ibid., p. 50.
58 EH, p. 85.
59 Nietzsche, *Untimely Meditations*, tr. R.J. Hollingdale (hereafter UM) Cambridge, 1983, p. 7.
60 UM, p. 8.
61 UM, p. 10; BT, 19.
62 BT, 15; UM, p. 27.
63 BT, 17; UM, p. 25.
64 BT, 23; UM, p. 33.
65 Arnold, *Culture*, p. 121.
66 BT, 1.
67 Ibid., 4.
68 Ibid., 3.
69 Ibid., 7.
70 Ibid., 6, and 1.
71 Ibid., 14.
72 See A. J. Greimas, 'The Interaction of Semiotic Constraints', in *On Meaning*, London, 1987, pp. 48–62. (See Figure.)
73 Plato, *Symposium*, 215.
74 BT, 15.
75 Ibid., p. 91.
76 J. Habermas, 'The Entwinement of Myth and Enlightenment: Re-reading *Dialectic of Enlightenment*', *New German Critique*, vol. 26, 1982, pp. 13–30.
77 Ibid., p. 36.
78 T. Adorno and M. Horkheimer, *Dialectic of Enlightenment*, tr. J. Cumming, London 1973, p. 32.
79 BT, 16.
80 Ibid., 12.
81 Ibid., 16; see also Adorno and Horkheimer, *Dialectic*, p. 32.
82 Adorno and Horkheimer, *Dialectic*, p. 33.

83 Ibid., p. 34.

84 Ibid., p. 46.

85 F. Nietzsche, *The Gay Science*, tr. W. Kaufmann, New York 1974 (hereafter GS), 372.

86 See, F. Jameson, *Late Marxism: Adorno, or, the Persistence of the Dialectic*, London, 1990, pp. 151–4.

87 Adorno and Horkheimer, *Dialectic*, p. 37.

88 Arnold, *Culture*, p. 50.

89 Ibid., p. 71.

90 BT, 13.

91 Ibid., 18.

92 Ibid., 15.

93 UM, p. 16.

94 GS, Pref. 2 (p. 35).

95 F. Nietzsche, *Beyond Good and Evil*, tr. W. Kaufmann, New York 1966 (hereafter BGE), 230.

96 K. Marx, *Early Writings*, tr. R. Livingstone and G. Benton, London, 1975, pp. 348–9.

97 Ibid., p. 358.

98 K. Marx, *Capital*, Vol. 1, tr. S. Moore and E. Aveling, New York, 1906, p. 837.

99 Marx, *Early Writings*, p. 357.

100 Ibid., p. 349.

101 K. Marx and F. Engels, *The German Ideology*, London 1976, p. 394. See also Taylor, *Art, an Enemy of the People*, pp. 55–87.

102 Marx, *Early Writings*, p. 329.

103 Ibid., p. 201.

104 Ibid., p. 327.

105 Ibid., p. 201.

106 Adorno, *Aesthetic Theory*, p. 52.

107 T. Eagleton, *The Ideology of the Aesthetic*, Oxford, 1990, p. 352.

108 BT, 12, and 14.

109 Ibid., 11.

110 GS, 125.

111   GS, 343.

112   Dante, *Inferno*, 26, 118–20.

113   Rilke, *Duino Elegies*, 8.

Anti-Nietzsche

1   Alain Boyer, 'Hierarchy and Truth', in L. Ferry and A. Renaut, eds., *Why We Are Not Nietzscheans*, Chicago, 1997, p. 2.

2   Geoff Waite, *Nietzsche's Corps/e: Aesthetics, Politics, Prophecy, or, The Spectacular Technology of Everyday Life*, Durham, NC, 1996, p. xi.

3   Ibid., p. 67 and p. 232.

4   Nietzsche quoted in ibid., pp. 315–6.

5   Fredrick Appel, *Nietzsche Contra Democracy*, Ithaca, 1999, p. 2.

6   F. Nietzsche, *The Will to Power* (hereafter WP), tr. W. Kaufmann and R. J. Hollingdale, New York, 1967, 872 (VII, 25.343). References to the *Will to Power* are followed by the corresponding reference in G. Colli and M. Montinari, eds., *Friedrich Nietzsche, Sämtliche Werke, Kritische Gesamtausgabe*, Berlin, 1967–77 (hereafter KGW), in the form: volume number, notebook number, note number.

7   D. Losurdo, *Nietzsche, il ribelle aristocratico*, Turin, 2002. On Socratism see especially chapters 1 and 3; on slavery chapter 12; on war, colonialism and extermination chapters 19, 22 and 23. On Nietzsche's plans for unfree labour, see also I. Landa, 'Nietzsche, the Chinese Worker's Friend', *New Left Review* 236, 1999, pp. 3–23.

8   J. Golomb and R. S. Wistrich, eds., *Nietzsche, Godfather of Fascism? On the Uses and Abuses of a Philosophy*, Princeton, 2002. But on nationalism and anti-Semitism see also Losurdo, *Nietzsche*, pp. 26–8 and 105–21.

9   WP, 958 (VII, 25.137).

10   Waite, *Nietzsche's Corps/e*, p. 24.

11   F. Nietzsche, *The Anti-Christ*, tr. R. J. Hollingdale, Harmondsworth, 1968 (hereafter abbreviated as A), Foreword (p. 114).

12 Wyndham Lewis, *The Art of Being Ruled*, Santa Rosa, CA, 1989, p. 113.

13 Stanley Rosen, *The Ancients and the Moderns*, New Haven, 1989, p. 190.

14 For the translation of *Übermensch* I have throughout preferred 'Superman' to Walter Kaufmann's 'Overman'. Though more literal, the latter is virtually meaningless in English. Little hangs on this, though 'Superman' does serve as a reminder of those connotations Kaufmann wished to play down, but which Nietzsche frequently sought to play up—e.g. in his identification of Cesare Borgia as a model for the type, see F. Nietzsche, *Twilight of the Idols*, tr. R. J. Hollingdale, Harmondsworth, 1968 (hereafter TI), p. 90 (37), EH, p. 71.

15 Daniel Conway, *Nietzsche's Dangerous Game: Philosophy in the Twilight of the Idols*, Cambridge, 1997, p. 152.

16 Ibid., p. 256.

17 See Keith Oatley, 'A Taxonomy of the Emotions in Literary Response and a Theory of Identification in Fictional Narrative', *Poetics*, 23, 1994, pp. 53–74; D. W. Allbritton and R. J. Gerrig found that readers have positive preferences for the outcomes of narratives, and that having negative preferences (e.g. hoping that the protagonist misses a flight) is so unusual that when readers are manipulated into preferring a negative outcome (e.g. by being told that the plane will crash) they are less able to remember the actual outcome; see their 'Participatory Responses in Text Understanding', *Journal of Memory and Language*, 30, 1991, pp. 603–26.

18 F. Nietzsche, *Human, All Too Human*, tr. R. J. Hollingdale, Cambridge, 1986 (hereafter HH), 1.621.

19 WP, 480 (VIII, 14.122).

20 WP, 643 (VIII, 2.148).

21 EH, p. 126.

22 Robert Burton, *The Anatomy of Melancholy*, Oxford, 1989, vol. 3, p. 434.

23 Ibid., p. 422.

24   F. Nietzsche, *On the Genealogy of Morals*, tr. D. Smith, Oxford, 1996 (hereafter GM), 3.14.

25   BGE, 185.

26   A, 1.

27   BT, 5; see also GS, 107.

28   BT, 5.

29   WP, 853 (VIII, 17.3).

30   WP, 821 (VIII, 14.47), and 809 (VIII, 14.119).

31   BGE 225.

32   WP, 812 (VIII, 14.119).

33   WP, 801 (VIII, 9.102).

34   F. Nietzsche, *Thus Spake Zarathustra*, tr. R. J. Hollingdale, Harmondsworth, 1969 (hereafter Z), p. 43.

35   Z, p. 41.

36   WP, 958 (VII, 25.137).

37   WP, 960 (VIII, 2.57).

38   WP, 943 (VII, 35.76).

39   GM, 1.13.

40   BGE, 203.

41   WP, Prologue, 3 (VIII, 11.411).

42   WP, 3 (VIII, 10.192).

43   M. Heidegger, *The Question Concerning Technology*, tr. W. Lovitt, New York, 1977, p. 67.

44   WP, 7 (VIII, 11.100).

45   WP, Prologue, 4 (VIII, 11.411).

46   WP, 12B (VIII, 11.99).

47   Heidegger, *Concerning Technology*, p. 70.

48   GM, Preface, 6.

49   WP, 221 (VIII, 11.363).

50   WP, 1006 (VIII, 10.89).

51   GM, 1.17n.

52   WP, 13 (VIII, 9.35).

53   TI, p. 45 (5.5).

54   WP, 55 (VIII, 5.71.10).

55 WP, 14 (VIII, 9.39).

56 WP, 713 (VIII, 14.8).

57 WP, 715 (VIII, 11.73).

58 BGE, 261.

59 GS, Pref. 2 (p. 35).

60 WP, 660 (VIII, 2.76).

61 WP, 960 (VIII, 2.57).

62 WP, 821 (VIII, 14.47).

63 WP, 94 (VII, 25.178).

64 WP, 315 (VIII, 9.173).

65 E. Durkheim, *The Division of Labour in Society*, tr. W. D. Halls, London, 1984, p. 117.

66 Ibid., p. 339.

67 BGE, 259.

68 Durkheim, *Division of Labour*, p. 337.

69 HH, 1.45; see also GM, 1.11.

70 Durkheim, *Division of Labour*, p. 209.

71 BGE, 258.

72 A, 61.

73 P. Cavalieri and P. Singer, eds., *The Great Ape Project*, London, 1993, p. 5 and p. 6.

74 See R. E. Goodin, C. Pateman and R. Pateman, 'Simian Sovereignty', *Political Theory*, 25, 1997, pp. 821–49.

75 On Nietzsche's fears for the Louvre at the hands of the Communards, see Losurdo, *Nietzsche*, p. 14.

Negative Ecologies

1 See Gillespie, *Nihilism Before Nietzsche*.

2 GS, 347; for a useful overview see S. Critchley, 'Travels in Nihilon', in *Very Little . . . Almost Nothing*, London, 1997, pp. 1–28.

3 *New York Times*, 24 April 1881.

4 J. Richepin, *Cauchemars*, Paris, 1892, p. 59.

5 WP, 1 (VIII, 2.127).

6   GM, Pref. 5 (translation modified).

7   WP, 1 (VIII, 2.127).

8   A, 58.

9   WP, 4, (VIII, 5.71.1); the quotation (and several of those that follow) comes from the Lenzer Heide fragment (VIII, 5.71), Nietzsche's most sustained reflection on nihilism, divided into four separate notes in *Will to Power*.

10 WP, 845 (VIII, 2.114).

11 GS, 346.

12 WP, 28 (VIII, 10.42).

13 WP, Pref. 4 (VIII, 11.411).

14 WP, 28 (VIII, 10.42).

15 WP, 13 (VIII, 9.35).

16 WP, 22, 23 (translation modified) (VIII, 9.35).

17 WP, 585 (VIII, 9.60).

18 WP, 866 (VIII, 10.17).

19 Other attempts to systematise the varieties of nihilism found in Nietzsche's thought include G. Deleuze, *Nietzsche and Philosophy*, tr. H. Tomlinson, London, 1983, p. 139 ff.; A. White, 'Nietzschean Nihilism: A Typology', *International Studies in Philosophy*, 19, 1987, pp. 29–44; E. Kuhn, *Friedrich Nietzsches Philosophie des europäischen Nihilismus*, Berlin, 1992; and B. Reginster, *The Affirmation of Life*, Cambridge, MA, 2006.

20 KGW, VIII, 11.280; EH, p. 79.

21 WP, 55 (VIII, 5.71.10,13).

22 WP, 114 and 55 (VIII, 5.71.3–4).

23 WP, 1 (VIII, 2.127).

24 A, 58 (see also WP 864), and WP 24 (11.123).

25 WP, 685 (VIII, 14.123).

26 GS, 347.

27 BT, 7; see also M. Müller, *Selected Essays*, London, 1881.

28 A, 20.

29 WP, 585 (VIII, 9.60).

30 A, 22.

31 WP, 64 (translation modified) (VIII, 9.82).

32 WP 23, (VIII, 9.35).

33 BGE, 202.

34 WP, 1 (translation modified) (VIII, 2.127).

35 WP, 458 (VIII, 14.107).

36 WP, 247 (VIII, 14.9).

37 WP, 55 (VIII, 5.71.12).

38 WP, 55 (VIII, 5.71.6)

39 BGE, 56.

40 WP, 55 (VIII, 5.71.14).

41 WP, 23, and VIII, 9.35.

42 WP, 585 (VIII, 9.60).

43 WP, 675 (VIII, 11.96), WP, 13 (VIII, 9.35).

44 WP, 55 (VIII, 5.71.15).

45 See for example, G. Vattimo, *Nihilism and Emancipation*, tr. S. Zabala, New York, 2004, p.54.

46 WP, 114 and 55 (VIII, 5.71.3,5,6).

47 WP, 749 (VIII, 10.94).

48 GM, Pref. 5; 2.24; Pref. 3.

49 WP, 112 (VIII, 10.22).

50 WP, 1041 (VIII, 16.32).

51 WP, 2 (VIII, 9.35).

52 WP, 675 and 55 (VIII, 11.96 and 5.71.10).

53 WP, 708 (VIII, 11.72).

54 WP, 711 (VIII, 11.74).

55 WP, 53 (VIII, 14.40).

56 WP, 708 (VIII, 11.72).

57 WP, 339 (VIII, 11.226).

58 EH, p. 129.

59 WP, 369 (VIII, 2.205).

60 WP, 660 (VIII, 2.76).

61 EH, p. 130; WP, 315 (VIII, 9.173).

62 GM, 2.12; cf. WP, 710 (VIII, 14.105).

63 EH, p. 129 (translation modified).

64   WP, 27 (VIII, 9.44).

65   WP, 37 (VIII, 9.107).

66   WP 55 (VIII, 5.71.14).

67   WP, 657 (VIII, 5.64).

68   VIII, 7.48.

69   WP, 56 (VIII, 11.150).

70   WP, 957 (VII, 37.8).

71   WP, 660 (VIII, 2.76).

72   WP, 859 (VIII, 7.6 (p. 289)).

73   WP, 866 (VIII, 10.17).

74   WP, 715 (translation modified) (VIII, 11.73).

75   KGW, VIII, 5.61; WP, 53 (VIII, 14.40).

76   WP, 715 (VIII, 11.73).

77   A, 55; GS, 358.

78   WP, 953 (translation modified) (VIII, 5.61).

79   Like the Prussian officer corps, or the Jesuits, WP, 796 (VIII, 2.114).

80   GM, 2.17 (translation modified); WP, 960 (VIII, 2.57).

81   WP, 960 (VIII, 2.57).

82   WP, 32 (VIII, 6.25).

83   BGE, 202.

84   WP, 125 (VII, 37.11).

85   BGE, 203.

86   WP, 872 (VII, 25.343).

87   WP, 713 (VIII, 14.8).

88   BGE, 203.

89   Z, pp. 46–7 (translation modified).

90   WP, 280 (VIII, 10.39).

91   WP, 285 (VII, 27.17).

92   BGE, 203; GM, 1.9 and 3.14.

93   BGE, 201.

94   WP, 50 (VIII, 16.53).

95   Z, p. 280.

96   UM, pp. 60–61.

Subhumanism

1   M. Heidegger, *Nietzsche*, 4 vols., tr. D. F. Krell, New York, 1979–87 (hereafter N1 etc.); 'The Word of Nietzsche: "God Is Dead"' in *The Question Concerning Technology* (hereafter 'Word'), pp. 53–112; 'Nihilism as Determined by the History of Being' (hereafter 'Nihilism') in N4, pp. 199–250; 'Letter on Humanism' in *Basic Writings*, ed. D. F. Krell (hereafter LH), pp. 217–65, and 'On the Question of Being' in *Pathmarks*, ed. W. McNeill, Cambridge, 1998 (hereafter QB), pp. 291–322. There is some variation in the capitalisation of 'Being' (*Sein*) between translations; I have capitalised throughout. In contrast, the capitalised spelling of 'nothing' is retained only in quotations.
2   'Word', p. 69.
3   N4, pp. 55–6.
4   N3, p. 207, and N4, p. 56.
5   'Word', p. 61.
6   'Word', pp. 65, 61–62.
7   N4, p. 5.
8   N3, p. 130 (cf. WP, 493 [VII, 34.253]), N3, p. 129.
9   N3, p. 25.
10   WP, 822 (VIII, 16 § 6) ('Word', p. 93).
11   N3, 124.
12   N3, 25.
13   'Word', p. 67.
14   'Word', p. 70 (WP, 14 [VIII, 9.39]).
15   'Word', p. 71; WP, 715 (translation modified) (VIII, 11.73).
16   'Word', p. 73.
17   N3, 195.
18   N3, p. 239.
19   'Word', pp. 85–6.
20   N4, pp. 67–8 (cf. 'Word', p. 81).
21   'Word', pp. 76–7.

22   N4, p. 31; see also, 'Word', p. 79 (cf. GM, 3.1).

23   N3, p. 234.

24   N2, p. 228; see also p. 257n.

25   N3, p. 156; WP, 617 (VIII, 7.54); cf. WP, 693 (VIII, 14.80).

26   N2, pp. 201–2.

27   'Nihilism', p. 202.

28   'Word', p. 110–111.

29   'Nihilism', pp. 200–1.

30   'Word', p. 56.

31   'Word', p. 82.

32   'Nihilism', p. 203.

33   'Nihilism', p. 201.

34   'Nihilism', p. 230.

35   'Nihilism', p. 219.

36   'Nihilism', pp. 208–9.

37   'Nihilism', p. 211.

38   N4, 169; 'Nihilism', p. 205.

39   'Word', p. 104.

40   'Nihilism', p. 220.

41   'Word', p. 110.

42   'Nihilism', p. 216.

43   'Nihilism', pp. 219, 228, 220.

44   'Nihilism', pp. 223, 222, 243.

45   'Nihilism', pp. 225 and 238–9.

46   'Nihilism', pp. 246 and 223–4

47   LH, p. 237 and 227.

48   LH, pp. 229, 228 and 237.

49   LH, p. 245.

50   LH, pp. 256–67 and p. 254.

51   QB, p. 309–10.

52   QB, p. 311.

53   QB, pp. 313, 314, 316.

54   LH, p. 233–4.

55   QB, p. 308.

56 M. Heidegger, *Parmenides*, tr. A. Schuwer and R. Rojcewicz, Bloomington, 1992, pp. 143 and 159.

57 LH, p. 230.

58 LH, pp. 217 and 252.

59 M. Heidegger, *The Fundamental Concepts of Metaphysics*, tr. W. McNeill and N. Walker, Bloomington, 1995 (hereafter FCM), pp. 193 and 269.

60 M. Heidegger, 'What Is Metaphysics?' in D. F. Krell, ed., *Basic Writings*, London, 1993, p. 109; M. Heidegger, *Introduction to Metaphysics*, tr. G. Fried and R. Polt, New Haven, 2000 (hereafter IM), p. 4.

61 QB, p. 317.

62 QB, p. 317.

63 See C. Bambach, *Heidegger's Roots: Nietzsche, National Socialism, and the Greeks*, Ithaca, 2003, p. 164, n. 76 and 77.

64 IM, p. 47 (cf. p. 40).

65 M. Heidegger, *Contributions to Philosophy*, tr. P. Emad and K. Maly, Bloomington, 1999, 56.15 and 13 (references are to section numbers).

66 M. Heidegger, *Introduction to Phenomenological Research*, tr. D. O. Dahlstrom, Bloomington, 2005, p. 7.

67 M. Heidegger, *Zollikon Seminars*, ed. M. Boss, Evanston, 2001, p. 13; cf. Heidegger, *Parmenides*, p. 61.

68 IM, p. 47.

69 J. Derrida, *Of Spirit: Heidegger and the Question*, tr. G. Bennington, Chicago, 1989, p. 59. See also J. Derrida, *The Animal That Therefore I Am*, tr. D. Wills, New York, 2008, pp. 141–60.

70 Heidegger, *Contributions*, 154 (translation modified); cf. FCM, p. 259.

71 FCM, p. 193.

72 FCM, p. 193.

73 FCM, pp. 284–5.

74 Derrida, *Of Spirit*, p. 49.

75 FCM, p. 272.

76   FCM, p. 271 (Rom. 8.19).

77   FCM, p. 202–3.

78   FCM, pp. 205–6.

79   FCM, pp. 204.

80   FCM, pp. 210–11.

81   IM, 4–6; see also F. Nietzsche, 'On Truth and Lies in a Nonmoral Sense' in K. Ansell Pearson and D. Large, eds., *The Nietzsche Reader*, Oxford, 2005, p. 114.

82   Heidegger, 'What Is Metaphysics?', p. 95.

83   IM, p. 41.

84   IM, p. 52.

85   IM, p. 219.

86   Heidegger, *Parmenides*, p. 160 (translation modified).

Excommunication

1   Hugo von Hofmannsthal, *The Lord Chandos Letter*, tr. J. Rotenberg, New York, 2005, pp. 120–1.

2   Ibid., p.122.

3   Ibid., p. 123.

4   Ibid., p. 124.

5   Ibid., p. 125.

6   G. Deleuze and F. Guattari, *A Thousand Plateaus*, tr. B. Massumi, Minneapolis, 1987, p. 258.

7   Ibid., pp. 241–2.

8   Hofmannsthal, *Chandos*, p. 127.

9   Ibid., p. 118.

10   Ibid., p. 121–2.

11   Ibid., p. 121.

12   Hermann Broch, *Hugo von Hofmannsthal and His Time*, tr. M. P. Steinberg, Chicago, 1984, p. 121.

13   FCM, p. 198, p. 247.

14   M. Heidegger, *Being and Time*, tr. J Macquarrie and E. Robinson, Oxford, 1962 (hereafter *Being*), p. 190.

15 Hofmannsthal, *Chandos*, pp. 121–2; cf. Rilke, *Duino Elegies*, VIII.

16 See Derrida, *Of Spirit*, p. 51.

17 FCM, p. 247.

18 FCM, p. 251.

19 Broch, *Hofmannsthal*, p. 122.

20 Hofmannsthal, *Chandos*, pp. 126 and 127.

21 FCM, pp. 248 and 259

22 Hofmannsthal, *Chandos*, pp. 127, 128.

23 FCM, pp. 202 and 203.

24 Deleuze and Guattari, *Thousand Plateaus*, pp. 241, 6–7.

25 Hofmannsthal, *Chandos*, p. 124.

26 A. Lingis, *The Community of Those Who Have Nothing in Common*, Bloomington, 1994, pp. 12–13, 10, 12–13.

27 J.-L. Nancy, *The Inoperative Community*, tr. P. Connor, Minneapolis, 1991, p. 28.

28 Ibid., p. xxxviii.

29 Ibid., p. 13.

30 Ibid., pp. 14, 15, 27, xxxix, 11.

31 J.-L. Nancy, '*La Comparution*/The Compearance: From the Existence of "Communism" to the Community of "Existence"', *Political Theory* 20, 1992, pp. 371–2.

32 J.-L Nancy, 'Of Being in Common', in Miami Theory Collective, eds., *Community at Loose Ends*, Minneapolis, 1991, p. 1.

33 J.-L. Nancy, *Being Singular Plural*, tr. R. D. Richardson and A. E. O'Byrne, Stanford, 2000 (hereafter BSP), p. 30 and p. 155.

34 Ibid., pp. 63 and 92.

35 J.-L. Nancy, 'Tre frammenti su nichilismo e politica', in R. Esposito, C. Galli and V. Vitiello, eds., *Nichilismo e politica*, Roma-Bari, 2000, pp. 11–12.

36 BSP, p. 18.

37 BSP, p. 99; cf. *Inoperative Community*, pp. 77–8.

38 *Being*, pp. 153–63.

39 FCM, pp. 206 and 210.

40 BSP, pp. 75 and 20.

41 BSP, p. 89.

42 Nancy, *Inoperative Community*, p. 33 (BT, pp. 282–83 [239]), and p. 15.

43 M. Heidegger, *Poetry, Language, Thought*, tr. A. Hofstadter, New York, 1976, pp. 178–9 (cf. *Being*, p. 290f).

44 BSP, p. 156.

45 BSP, p. 5.

46 FCM, p. 196-97.

47 *Being*, p. 81.

48 *Being*, p. 282.

49 FCM, p. 198.

50 Derrida, *Of Spirit*, pp. 52–3.

51 BSP, pp. 90, 93, and 28.

52 LH, p. 230.

53 BSP, p. 88; cf. G. Agamben, *Coming Community*, tr. M. Hardt, Minneapolis, 1993, pp. 98–100.

54 *Being*, pp. 207 and 189.

55 FCM, p. 307.

56 Broch, *Hofmannsthal*, p. 165.

57 L. Wittgenstein, *Tractatus Logico-Philosophicus*, tr. D.F. Pears and B. F. McGuiness, London, 1961, 7.

58 Nancy, *Inoperative Community*, pp. 50–1.

59 BSP, p. 90.

60 Nancy, *Inoperative Community*, p. 62.

61 Ibid., pp. 63, 62, 68–9.

62 BT, 7, 1, 17.

63 BT, 25, 16.

64 BT, 13; cf. Goethe, *Faust*, 1607–11.

65 BT, 13, 23 (p. 136).

66 See Nancy, '*La Comparution*', p. 374.

67 BT, 14 and Z, p. 104; Heidegger, 'Nihilism and the History of Being', p. 238; BSP, p. 37.

68 BT, 7; cf. WP, 1050 (VIII, 14.14).

69 Hofmannsthal, *Chandos*, pp. 120 and 122.

70 Ibid., p. 126.

71 A. Kojève, *Introduction to the Reading of Hegel*, tr. J. H. Nichols, New York, 1969, p. 159n.

72 Hofmannsthal, *Chandos*, p. 128.

73 Nancy, '*La Comparution*', p. 372.

74 Heidegger, *Parmenides*, p. 153.

75 G. Agamben, *The Open: Man and Animal*, tr. K. Attell, Stanford, 2004, p. 3.

76 J.-L. Nancy, *The Birth to Presence*, tr. B. Holmes et al., Stanford, 1993, p. 44.

77 Nancy, '*La Comparution*', p. 372.

78 Nancy, *Birth to Presence*, p. 47.

79 G. Agamben, *Homo Sacer*, tr. D. Heller-Roazen, Stanford, 1998, pp. 59–60.

80 Ibid., p. 60 and pp. 109–10.

81 G. Agamben, *Remnants of Auschwitz: The Witness and the Archive*, tr. D. Heller-Roazen, New York, 1999, pp. 41 (quoting Jean Améry) and 78.

82 Agamben, *The Open*, p. 38.

83 Agamben, *Remnants*, pp. 74, 80–1.

84 Ibid., p. 59.

85 Agamben, *Coming Community*, p. 39.

86 Ibid., pp. 90, 103, and 90.

87 Agamben, *Open*, p. 90.

88 Agamben, *Coming Community*, p. 40.

89 Agamben, *Open*, p. 92.

90 Ibid., p. 90; cf. *Coming Community*, p. 93.

91 FCM, p. 273 (cf. Romans 8.19); Agamben, *Coming Community*, pp. 40 and 141 (cf. W. Benjamin, *One-Way Street*, tr. E. Jephcott and K. Shorter, London, 1979, p. 156).

92 Agamben, *Coming Community*, p. 102.

93 G. Agamben, *The Man Without Content*, tr. G. Albert, Stanford, 1999, p. 56.

94 EH, p. 45.

95 WP, 866 (VIII, 10.17).

96 A, 57.

97 IM, pp. 47, 50–1, and 49.

98 E. Durkheim, *Pragmatism and Sociology*, tr. J. B. Allcock, Cambridge, 1983, pp. 91 and 88.

99 Ibid., pp. 91–2.

100 Durkheim, *Division of Labour*, p. 298.

101 Ibid., pp. 304–5 and 306.

102 Ibid., pp. 207 and 294.

103 BSP, p. 92.

104 M. Serres, *The Parasite*, tr. L. R. Schehr, Minneapolis, 2007, pp. 123 and 121; G. E. Leibniz, *The Leibniz-Arnauld Correspondence*, tr. H. T. Mason, Manchester, 1967, p. 119.

105 Serres, *Parasite*, p. 123.

106 FCM, p. 198.

107 Durkheim, *Division of Labour*, p. 209.

108 Hofmannsthal, *Chandos*, p. 126.

109 See M. Heidegger, *The Metaphysical Foundations of Logic*, tr. M. Heim, Bloomington, 1984, pp. 70–100 (86–123).

Counter-Interest

1 F. Nietzsche, 'The Dionysiac World View', in R. Geuss and R. Speirs, eds., *The Birth of Tragedy and Other Writings*, Cambridge, 1999, p. 132; F. Nietzsche, Daybreak, tr. R. J. Hollingdale, Cambridge, 1982 (hereafter D), 531.

2 D, 271.

3 Z, p. 177.

4 Z, p. 48.

5 GS, 125 (translation modified).

6 BGE, 193.

7 GM, 3.25.

8 GM, 3.25. and Z, p. 48.

9 WP, 857 (VIII, 15.120); also WP, 339 (VIII, 11.226).

10 TI, p. 85.

11   WP, 373 (VIII, 14.29).
12   For instance, WP, 942 (VII, 41.3).
13   GM, 3.14.
14   GM, 1.7.
15   BGE, 257.
16   BGE, 259.
17   GS, 377.
18   GS, 118.
19   Z, p. 229
20   TI, p. 86.
21   TI, p. 57.
22   TI, p. 56.
23   GM, 3.14.
24   BGE, 62.
25   GS, 14; cf. 118.
26   GS, 118 and 13.
27   GS, 13.
28   D, 142.
29   HH, 1.50.
30   WP, 368 (VIII, 7.4).
31   A, 7.
32   A, 7.
33   A, 7; see also GM, Pref. 5.
34   BGE, 293.
35   WP, 83 (VIII, 9.182), 270 (VIII, 10.121), and 1017 S (VIII, 10.5).
36   D, 137; HH, 1. 57.
37   WP, 276 (VIII, 5.35); WP, 389 (VIII, 7.6).
38   BGE, 222.
39   BGE, 293.
40   BGE, 260; cf. BGE, 199.
41   WP, 864 (VIII, 14.182).
42   GM, 3.15.
43   BGE, 260.
44   WP, 367 (VII, 36.7).

45 WP, 119 (VIII, 10.119).

46 BGE, 225.

47 Z, p. 226.

48 D, 136 and 135.

49 A. Schopenhauer, *The World as Will and Representation*, 2 vols., tr. E. F. J. Payne (hereafter WWR), New York, 1969, vol. 1, p. 309.

50 A. Schopenhauer, *On the Basis of Morality*, tr. E. F. J. Payne, Indianapolis, 1995, pp. 145 and 144.

51 Ibid., 143.

52 WWR1, pp. 378–9.

53 Ibid., pp. 379, 301, and 378.

54 Ibid., pp. 376, 379, and 390.

55 Ibid., p. 196.

56 BGE, 33 and 220.

57 GM, 3.6.

58 GM, 3.6.

59 WP, 84 (VIII, 14.219).

60 WP, 84 (VIII, 14.219).

61 WWR2, p. 213.

62 WP, 84 (VIII, 14.219).

63 WP, 46 (VIII, 14.219); cf. WP, 692 (VIII, 14.121).

64 WP, 689 (VIII, 14.82).

65 WP, 46 (VIII, 14.219).

66 TI, p. 43.

67 EH, pp. 43–4; D, 134.

68 Aristotle, *Nicomachean Ethics*, 7.7.

69 BGE, 260 (cf. D,133); Z, pp. 174 and 231.

70 WP, 179 (VIII, 11.240); WP, 395 (VIII, 4.7); WP, 1021 (VIII, 10.2).

71 BGE, 212.

72 BGE, 201.

73 GM, 3.17.

74 A, 20.

75 WP, 279 (VIII, 7.6); WP, 355 (VIII, 1.25); cf. WP, 864 (VIII, 14.182). F. de La Rochefoucauld, *Maxims*, 237.

76 D, 174; WP, 868 (VIII, 11.31).

77 T. E. Wilkerson, *Irrational Action: A Philosophical Analysis*, Aldershot, 1997, p. 161.

78 J.-P. Sartre, *Being and Nothingness*, tr. H. E. Barnes, London, 1958, p. 608.

79 G. Vattimo, *Beyond Interpretation*, tr. D. Webb, Oxford, 1996, p. 12; cf. BGE, 22.

80 Vattimo, *Nihilism and Emancipation*, p. 146.

81 Vattimo, *Beyond Interpretation*, pp. 13 and 140–1.

82 Vattimo, *Nihilism and Emancipation*, p. 20.

83 G. Vattimo, *Dialogue with Nietzsche*, tr. W. McCuaig, New York, 2006, p. 131.

84 Ibid., p. 140.

85 Vattimo, *Nihilism and Emancipation*, p. 20.

86 See chapter 3.

87 WP, 643 (VIII, 2.148).

88 WP, 556 (VIII, 2.151).

89 WP, 48 (VIII, 14.68).

90 G. Vattimo, 'Hermeneutics and Nihilism: An Apology for Aesthetic Consciousness', in B. R. Wachterhauser, ed., *Hermeneutics and Modern Philosophy*, Albany, 1986, p. 453.

91 G. Vattimo, *The End of Modernity: Nihilism and Hermeneutics in Post-modern Culture*, tr. J. R. Snyder, Cambridge, 1988, pp. 114–15; cf. 'Hermeneutics and Nihilism', pp. 447 and 459.

92 Vattimo, *Dialogue with Nietzsche*, p. 140.

93 Vattimo, *Nihilism and Emancipation*, p. 55.

94 Schopenhauer, WWR1, pp. 390 and 197.

95 TI, p. 72.

96 UM, pp. 13 and 53.

The Great Beast

1   GM, 1.4.

2   BGE, 44; Z, p. 124.

3   TI, p. 102 (48); Z, p. 124.

4.   TI, p. 102 (48)

5   GM, 1.11.

6   HH, 1.45.

7   D, 174; cf. Z, p. 189.

8   WP, 603 (VII, 35.47).

9   WP, 2 (VIII, 9.35).

10   GM, 2.11.

11   WP, 246 (VIII, 15.110).

12   WP, 208 (VIII, 11.155).

13   A, 43.

14   O. Le Cour Grandmaison, *Les citoyennetés en révolution*, Paris, 1992, pp. 81–2.

15   S. Maréchal, 'Le Manifeste des Egaux', in P. Buonarroti, *La Conspiration pour l'égalité, dite de Babeuf*, Paris, 1957, vol. 2, pp. 94–8.

16   Ibid.

17   G. Babeuf, *La guerre de la Vendée*, Paris, 1987, pp. 90–6.

18   P. J. Proudhon, *What is Property?*, tr. D. R. Kelley and B. G. Smith, Cambridge, 1994, p. 100.

19   Ibid., p. 197.

20   Marx, *Early Writings*, p. 346.

21   J. Elster, ed., *Marx: A Reader*, Cambridge, 1986, p. 270.

22   See G. Stedman Jones, 'Introduction', in K. Marx and F. Engels, *Communist Manifesto*, London, 2002, pp. 162–76, drawing on I. Hont, 'Negative Community: the Natural Law Heritage from Pufendorf to Marx' (unpublished paper, 1989).

23   S. Pufendorf, *De jure naturae et gentium libri octo*, vol. 2, tr. C. H. Oldfather and W. A. Oldfather, Oxford, 1934, p. 535.

24   Proudhon, *What Is Property?*, p. 196; Marx, *Early Writings*, p. 347.

25 Elster, ed., *Marx: A Reader*, p. 166.

26 S. Dolgoff, ed., *Bakunin on Anarchy*, London, 1973, pp. 294 and 117.

27 Ibid., pp. 327, 129, and 136.

28 Ibid., p. 378.

29 L. Trotsky, *The Permanent Revolution*, London, 2007, p. 166.

30 Ibid., pp. 117–20 and 119.

31 Pufendorf, *De jure naturae*, p. 554.

32 GS, 111; Nietzsche, 'On Truth and Lies', p. 117; WP, 810 (VIII, 10.60); WP, 499 (VII, 41.11).

33 WP, 511 (VIII, 2.90).

34 WP, 501 (VIII, 5.65); cf. WP, 510 (VIII, 7.9).

35 WP, 509 (VIII, 7.41).

36 GM, Pref. 4; cf. D, 112.

37 Nietzsche, *The Wanderer and his Shadow*, tr. R.J. Hollingdale, Cambridge, 1986 (hereafter WS), 26.

38 WS, 22.

39 TI, pp. 85–6 (33); TI, p. 88 (36).

40 A further possibility, not systematically developed, is that the presence of the weak might serve to inoculate the strong against weakness, HH, 1.224; even socialism might perform this function, WP, 125 (VII, 37.11), and WP, 132 (VII, 35.9).

41 GM, 2.10; see also D, 202.

42 BGE, 201.

43 WP, 50 (VIII, 16.53).

44 The classic statements of the 'levelling down objection', the 'repugnant conclusion', and the 'tragedy of the commons' are, respectively, D. Parfit, 'Equality and Priority', in A. Mason, ed., *Ideals of Equality*, Oxford, 1998, pp. 1–20; D. Parfit, *Reasons and Persons*, Oxford, 1984, pp. 381–90; and G. Hardin, 'The Tragedy of the Commons', *Science* 162 (1968), pp. 1243–48.

45 Parfit, *Reasons and Persons*, pp. 419–41, and D. Parfit, 'Overpopulation and the Quality of Life', in J. Ryberg and T. Tännsjö, eds., *The Repugnant Conclusion*, Dordrecht, 2004, pp. 7–22.

46 WS, 263.

47 T. Nagel, *Equality and Partiality*, Oxford, 1991, pp. 135, 132, and 138.

48 Parfit, 'Overpopulation', pp. 19–20.

49 Nagel, *Equality*, p. 130.

50 S. Weil, *Gravity and Grace*, tr. E. Crawford and M. von der Ruhr, London, 2002, 167.

51 GM, 3.25.

52 Not only morally, but sociologically; see S. Weil, *The Need for Roots*, tr. A. Wills, London, 1952, pp. 16–19.

53 S. Weil, *On Science, Necessity, and the Love of God*, tr. R. Rees, Oxford, 1968, p. 79.

54 Weil, *Gravity*, p. 166; cf. Nietzsche's 'society of anarchists', WP, 739 (VIII 14.197), and Bayle's 'society of atheists' in chapter one.

55 S. Weil, *The Notebooks*, vol. 1, tr. A. Wills, London, 2004, p. 505.

56 Plato, *Republic*, 6.493.

57 S. Weil, *Oppression and Liberty*, tr. A. Wills and J. Petrie, London, 1958, p. 172; cf. *Gravity*, p. 167.

58 E. Durkheim, *The Rules of Sociological Method*, ed. W. D. Halls, New York, 1982, p. 102. Socrates, whom Nietzsche also likened to a criminal (TI, p. 30) is cited as an example.

59 D, 206.

60 G. D'Annunzio, *Prose di romanzi*, Milan, 1989, p. 29.

61 G. D'Annunzio, 'The Beast Who Wills' (sic), tr. J. Schnapp, in T. Harrison, ed, *Nietzsche in Italy*, Saratoga, CA, 1988, pp. 274–7.

62 T. Browne, *Major Works*, Harmondsworth, 1977, p. 134.

63 Vincenzo Cuoco, *Saggio storico sulla rivoluzione di Napoli*, 2nd ed., Milan, 1820, p. 102.

64 Ibid., p. 171.

65 Ibid., p. 114.

66 W. Carridi, ed., *Il pensiero politico e pedagogico di Vincenzo Cuoco*, Lecce, 1981, p. 250.

67 Carridi, ed., p. 253.

68　A. Gramsci, *Selections from the Prison Notebooks*, tr. Q. Hoare and G. Nowell Smith, London, 1971, p. 108.

69　Ibid., p. 79–80 n.

70　Ibid., p. 59.

71　Ibid., p. 110.

72　A. Gramsci, *Quaderni del carcere*, vol. 2, Turin, 1975, p. 973.

73　Gramsci, *Selections*, p. 80 n.

74　Ibid., p. 243. See further P. Anderson, 'The Antinomies of Antonio Gramsci', *New Left Review*, 100, 1976, pp. 5–78.

75　Ibid., p. 108.

76　Ibid., p. 260.

77　Ibid., p. 238.

Index

On the Typeface

Anti-Nietzsche is set in Monotype Fournier, a typeface based on the designs of the eighteenth-century printer and typefounder Pierre Simon Fournier. He in turn was influenced by the constructed type designs of the Romain du Roi, commissioned by Louis XIV in 1692, which eschewed the calligraphic influence of prior typefaces in favour of scientific precision and adherence to a grid.

With its vertical axis, pronounced contrast and unbracketed serifs, the Fournier face is an archetype of the 'transitional' style in the evolution of Latin printing types—situated between the 'old style' fonts such as Bembo and Garamond and the 'modern' faces of Bodoni and Didot. Other distinguishing features include the proportionally low height of the capitals and the lowercase 'f', with its tapered and declining crossbar.

The italics, which were designed independently, have an exaggerated slope with sharp terminals that retain the squared serifs in the descenders.

The Fournier design was commissioned as part of the Monotype Corporation's type revival programme under the supervision of Stanley Morison in the 1920s. Two designs were cut based on the 'St Augustin Ordinaire' design shown in Fournier's *Manuel Typographique*. In Morison's absence, the wrong design was approved, resulting in the typeface now known as Fournier.